PowerScore®
LSAT
GAME TYPE
TRAINING

VOLUME 1: LSAT PREPTESTS 1 THROUGH 20

The complete text of every LSAT Logic Game from
PrepTest 1 through 20 sorted according to
PowerScore's famous LSAT Logic Games Bible system.

POWERSCORE®
TEST PREPARATION

Published by
PowerScore Publishing, a division of PowerScore Incorporated
57 Hasell Street
Charleston, SC 29401

Author: David M. Killoran

Manufactured in Canada
09 15 20 16

ISBN: 978-0-9826618-2-6

MIX
Paper from
responsible sources
FSC® C004071

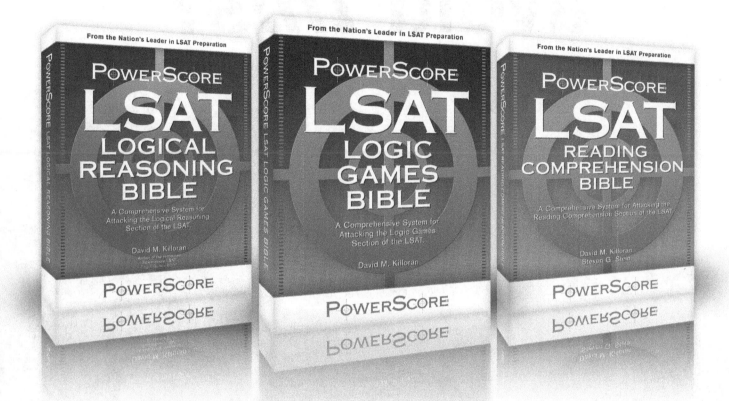

How will you avoid *this*?

 First Choice Law School Admissions

Dear Applicant,

We regret to inform you that after careful consideration, the Admissions Committee has declined your application for admission to First Choice University Law School.

During this admission season, approximately 10,000 candidates have applied for an entering class that is limited to 200 students. We hope that you will understand that this decision is the direct result of our exceptionally strong applicant pool, and is not a reflection of your potential to be a successful law student. We must select for admission those whom we believe to be the very best of an outstanding group, and it pains us to deny admission to many whom we would like to have at First Choice.

Thank you for your interest in First Choice, and I am sorry that the Committee could not act favorably on your application.

Sincerely,

Assistant Dean for Admissions

CONTENTS

CHAPTER ONE: INTRODUCTION

CHAPTER TWO: BASIC LINEAR GAMES

CHAPTER THREE: ADVANCED LINEAR GAMES

CHAPTER FOUR: GROUPING GAMES

CHAPTER FIVE: GROUPING/LINEAR COMBINATION GAMES

CHAPTER SIX: PURE SEQUENCING GAMES

CHAPTER SEVEN: THE FORGOTTEN FEW

PATTERN GAMES

CIRCULAR LINEARITY GAMES

MAPPING GAMES

Chapter Eight: Advanced Features and Techniques

Answer Key

Appendix

About PowerScore

PowerScore is one of the nation's fastest growing test preparation companies. Founded in 1997, PowerScore offers LSAT, GMAT, GRE, SAT, and ACT preparation classes in over 150 locations in the U.S. and abroad. Preparation options include Full-length courses, Weekend courses, Live Online courses, and private tutoring. For more information, please visit our website at www.powerscore.com or call us at (800) 545-1750.

For supplemental information about this book, please visit the *Game Type Training* website at www.powerscore.com/lsatbibles. The website contains additions to the text and answers to questions submitted by students.

Chapter One:
Introduction

Chapter One: Practice Drills

Welcome to *LSAT Game Type Training* by PowerScore. In this book you will find every Logic Game from LSAT PrepTests 1 through 20, arranged in groups according to the classification system used in the renowned *PowerScore LSAT Logic Games Bible*, and presented in the same order for easy cross-reference (for example, Grouping Games are covered in Chapter Four of this book and in Chapter Four of the *Logic Games Bible*).

Grouping each game by type provides a number of practical benefits:

- The 80 games in this book are an excellent practice resource, and an ideal supplement to the *LSAT Logic Games Bible* and *LSAT Logic Games Bible Workbook*.

- Grouping the games by classification provides practice with specific types of games, allowing particular focus on the game types you find most challenging.

- By examining games with certain basic similarities, you can analyze the features of each game type in order to better understand how games are constructed, how they can be most easily recognized, and how they can best be solved. This is especially the case if you have already read the *PowerScore LSAT Logic Games Bible*.

- Alternatively, for more general practice with games of all types, you can use the appendix in the back of the book and do complete game sections from individual tests. The appendix on page 125 gives directions for taking that approach.

- Even if you have not read the *LSAT Logic Games Bible*, this book provides an excellent practice resource, allowing you to develop your familiarity with various game types and with the Logic Games section in general.

At the end of this book a complete answer key is provided; however, no setups or explanations are given. For complete setups and explanations to all 80 games, as well as full explanations for all 480 questions, please see our sister publication, the *PowerScore LSAT Logic Games Setups Encyclopedia*.

If you are looking to further improve your LSAT score, we also recommend that you pick up copies of the renowned PowerScore LSAT Logical Reasoning Bible and LSAT Reading Comprehension Bible. When combined with the Logic Games Bible, you will have a formidable methodology for attacking the test. The other LSAT Bibles are available through our website at powerscore.com and at fine retailers.

In our LSAT courses, our admissions counseling programs, and in our publications, we always strive to present the most accurate and up-to-date information available. Consequently, we have devoted a section of our website to *LSAT Game Type Training* students. This free online resource area offers supplements to the book material, answers questions posed by students, offers study plans, and provides updates as needed. There is also an official book evaluation form that we strongly encourage you to use. The exclusive *LSAT Game Type Training* online area can be accessed at:

 **powerscore.com/lsatbibles**

If you wish to ask questions about items in this book, please visit our free LSAT discussion forum at:

 **forum.powerscore.com/lsat**

The forum offers hundreds of answers to student questions, including many lengthy answers and conceptual discussions from the author of this book.

If you have an issue that you prefer not to discuss on the public forum, please do not hesitate to email us at:

 **lsatbibles@powerscore.com**

We are happy to assist you in your LSAT preparation in any way, and we look forward to hearing from you!

A Brief Overview of the LSAT

The Law School Admission Test is administered four times a year: in February, June, September/October, and December. This standardized test is required for admission to any American Bar Association-approved law school. According to LSAC, the producers of the test, the LSAT is designed "to measure skills that are considered essential for success in law school: the reading and comprehension of complex texts with accuracy and insight; the organization and management of information and the ability to draw reasonable inferences from it; the ability to think critically; and the analysis and evaluation of the reasoning and arguments of others." The LSAT consists of the following five sections:

- 2 Sections of Logical Reasoning (short arguments, 24-26 questions each)

- 1 Section of Reading Comprehension (3 long reading passages, 2 short comparative reading passages, 26-28 total questions)

- 1 Section of Analytical Reasoning (4 logic games, 22-24 total questions)

- 1 Experimental Section of one of the above three section types.

You are given 35 minutes to complete each section. The experimental section is unscored and is not returned to the test taker. A break of 10 to 15 minutes is given between the 3rd and 4th sections.

The five-section test is followed by a 35-minute writing sample.

The Logical Reasoning Section

Each Logical Reasoning Section is composed of approximately 24 to 26 short arguments. Every short argument is followed by a question such as: "Which one of the following weakens the argument?", "Which one of the following parallels the argument?", or "Which one of the following must be true according to the argument?". The key to this section is time management and an understanding of the reasoning types and question types that frequently appear.

Since there are two scored sections of Logical Reasoning on every LSAT, this section accounts for approximately 50% of your score.

At the conclusion of the LSAT, and for five business days afterwards, you have the option of cancelling your score. Unfortunately, there is no way to determine exactly what your score would be before cancelling.

The Analytical Reasoning Section

This section, also known as Logic Games, is probably the most difficult for students taking the LSAT for the first time. The section consists of four games or puzzles, each followed by a series of five to eight questions. The questions are designed to test your ability to evaluate a set of relationships and to make inferences about those relationships. To perform well on this section you must understand the types of games that frequently appear and develop the ability to properly diagram the rules and make inferences.

The Reading Comprehension Section

This section is composed of three long reading passages, each approximately 450 words in length, and two shorter comparative reading passages. The passage topics are drawn from a variety of subjects, and each passage is followed by a series of five to eight questions that ask you to determine viewpoints in the passage, analyze organizational traits, evaluate specific sections of the passage, or compare facets of two different passages.

The Experimental Section

Each LSAT contains one undesignated experimental section, and it does not count towards your score. The experimental can be any of the three section types previously discussed, and the purpose of the section is to test and evaluate questions that will be used on *future* LSATs. By pretesting questions before their use in a scored section, the experimental helps the makers of the test determine the test scale.

The Writing Sample

For many years the Writing Sample was administered before the LSAT.

A 35-minute Writing Sample is given at the conclusion of the LSAT. The Writing Sample is not scored, but a copy is sent to each of the law schools to which you apply. In the Writing Sample you are asked to write a short essay that defends one of two possible courses of action.

You must attempt the Writing Sample! If you do not, LSAC reserves the right not to score your test.

Do not agonize over the Writing Sample; in law school admissions, the Writing Sample is not a major determining element for three reasons: the admissions committee is aware that the essay is given after a grueling three hour test and is about a subject you have no personal interest in; they already have a better sample of your writing ability in the personal statement; and the committee has a limited amount of time to evaluate each application.

The LSAT Scoring Scale

Each administered LSAT contains approximately 101 questions, and each LSAT score is based on the total number of questions a test taker correctly answers, a total known as the raw score. After the raw score is determined, a unique Score Conversion Chart is used for each LSAT to convert the raw score into a scaled LSAT score. Since June 1991, the LSAT has used a 120 to 180 scoring scale, with 120 being the lowest possible score and 180 being the highest possible score. Notably, this 120 to 180 scale is just a renumbered version of the 200 to 800 scale most test takers are familiar with from the SAT and GMAT. Just drop the "1" and add a "0" to the 120 and 180.

Although the number of questions per test has remained relatively constant over the last eight years, the overall logical difficulty of each test has varied. This is not surprising since the test is made by humans and there is no precise way to completely predetermine logical difficulty. To account for these variances in test "toughness," the test makers adjust the Scoring Conversion Chart for each LSAT in order to make similar LSAT scores from different tests mean the same thing. For example, the LSAT given in June may be logically more difficult than the LSAT given in December, but by making the June LSAT scale "looser" than the December scale, a 160 on each test would represent the same level of performance. This scale adjustment, known as equating, is extremely important to law school admissions offices around the country. Imagine the difficulties that would be posed by unequated tests: admissions officers would have to not only examine individual LSAT scores, but also take into account which LSAT each score came from. This would present an information nightmare.

The LSAT Percentile Table

It is important not to lose sight of what LSAT scaled scores actually represent. The 120 to 180 test scale contains 61 different possible scores. Each score places a student in a certain relative position compared to other test takers. These relative positions are represented through a percentile that correlates to each score. The percentile indicates where the test taker ranks in the overall pool of test takers. For example, a score of 165 represents the 93rd percentile, meaning a student with a score of 165 scored better than 93 percent of the people who have taken the test in the last three years. The percentile is critical since it is a true indicator of your positioning relative to other test takers, and thus law school applicants.

Charting out the entire percentage table yields a rough "bell curve." The number of test takers in the 120s and 170s is very low (only 1.6% of all test takers receive a score in the 170s), and most test takers are bunched in the middle, comprising the "top" of the bell. In fact, approximately 40% of all test takers score between 145 and 155 inclusive, and about 70% of all test takers score between 140 and 160 inclusive.

Since the LSAT has 61 possible scores, why didn't the test makers change the scale to 0 to 60? Probably for merciful reasons. How would you tell your friends that you scored a 3 on the LSAT? 123 sounds so much better.

The median score on the LSAT scale is approximately 151. The median, or middle, score is the score at which approximately 50% of test takers have a lower score and 50% of test takers have a higher score. Typically, to achieve a score of 151, you must answer between 56 and 61 questions correctly from a total of 101 questions. In other words, to achieve a score that is perfectly average, you can miss between 40 and 45 questions. Thus, it is important to remember that you don't have to answer every question correctly in order to receive an excellent LSAT score. There is room for error, and accordingly you should never let any single question occupy an inordinate amount of your time.

The Use of the LSAT

The use of the LSAT in law school admissions is not without controversy. It is largely taken for granted that your LSAT score is one of the most important determinants of the type of school you can attend. At many law schools a multiplier made up of your LSAT score and your undergraduate grade point average is used to help determine the relative standing of applicants, and at some schools a sufficiently high multiplier guarantees your admission.

For all the importance of the LSAT, it is not without flaws. As a standardized test currently given in the paper-and-pencil format, there are a number of skills that the LSAT cannot measure, such as listening skills, note-taking ability, perseverance, etc. LSAC is aware of these limitations and as a matter of course they warn all law schools about overemphasizing LSAT results. Still, since the test ultimately returns a number for each student, it is hard to escape the tendency to rank applicants accordingly. Fortunately, once you get to law school the LSAT is forgotten. Consider the test a temporary hurdle you must leap in order to reach the ultimate goal.

For more information on the LSAT, or to register for the test, contact LSAC at (215) 968-1001 or at their website at www.lsac.org.

The Analytical Reasoning Section

As you know, the focus of this book is on the Analytical Reasoning section. Each Analytical Reasoning section contains four games and a total of 22-24 questions. Since you have thirty-five minutes to complete the section, you have an average of eight minutes and forty-five seconds to complete each game. Of course, the amount of time you spend on each game will vary with the difficulty and the number of questions per game. For many students, the time constraint is what makes Logic Games the most difficult section on the LSAT, and as we progress through this book, we will discuss time management techniques as well as timesaving techniques that you can employ within the section.

On average, you have 8 minutes and 45 seconds to complete each game.

Each logic game contains three separate parts: the scenario, the rules, and the questions.

The Scenario

The game scenario introduces a group of variables—people, places, things, or events—involved in an easy-to-understand activity such as sitting in seats or singing songs. Here is a game scenario example:

> Seven comics—Janet, Khan, Leticia, Ming, Neville, Olivia, and Paul—will be scheduled to perform in the finals of a comedy competition. During the evening of the competition, each comic, performing alone, will give exactly one performance.

In the above scenario there are two variable sets: the comics J, K, L, M, N, O, and P, and the seven performance positions, which would be numbered 1 through 7.

Always write down and keep track of each variable set.

In basic terms, the scenario "sets the table" for the game and provides you with a quick picture of the situation to be analyzed. Although many game scenarios simply introduce the variables, on occasion the test makers place numerical information in the scenario, and this information is critical to understanding the possibilities inherent in the game.

Because you cannot afford to misunderstand any of the basics of the game, you must read the game scenario very closely.

The Rules

The second part of every game is the rules—a set of statements that describe and control the relationships between the variables. Here are the rules that accompany the above game scenario:

> Neville performs either second or sixth.
> Paul performs at some time after Leticia performs.
> Janet performs at some time after Khan performs.
> There is exactly one performance between Neville's performance and Olivia's performance, whether or not Neville performs before Olivia performs.

The initial rules apply to every question unless otherwise indicated.

Each of the initial rules in a game applies to each and every question; however, on occasion a question will explicitly suspend one or more rules for the purposes of that question only. These "suspension" questions always occur at the end of the game.

The third and final part of each logic game is a set of approximately five to eight questions that test your knowledge of the relationships between the variables, the structural features of the game, and the way those relationships and features change as conditions in the game change. More on the questions in a moment.

Approaching the Games

Always read through the entire scenario and each rule before you begin diagramming.

As you begin each game you should carefully and completely read through the entire game scenario and all of the rules *before* you begin writing. This initial reading will help you determine the type of game you are facing, as well as what variable sets exist and what relationships govern their actions. This advice will save you time by allowing you to formulate an exact plan of action, and it will save you from diagramming a rule and then re-diagramming if you find a later rule that alters the situation. At this point in the game you must also fix the rules in your memory. Students who fail to identify strongly with the rules inevitably struggle with the questions. It is also important to identify the most powerful rules in a game and to consider how the rules interact with one another. Of course, we will discuss how to do this throughout our analysis.

In general, these are the initial steps you must take to efficiently move through each game:

1. Read through and fix the rules in your mind.
2. Diagram the scenario and the rules.
3. Make inferences.
4. Use the rules and inferences to attack the questions.

Setups and Diagramming

Your initial reading of the game will also indicate what setup to use to attack the game. Many students are not aware of the best ways to set up logic games, and waste far too much time during the actual exam wondering what approach to take. Because you must read the rules and set up a diagram quickly and efficiently, the key to succeeding on the Logic Games section is to know the ideal approach to every game type before walking into the exam.

You should use the space at the bottom of each game page to diagram your initial setup. This setup should include:

Make a main diagram at the bottom of the page.

1. A list of the variables and their number.
    For example: J K L M N O P ^{7}

2. An identification of any randoms in the game (randoms are variables that do not appear in any rules).

3. A diagrammatic representation of the variable sets.

4. A diagrammatic representation of the rules.

5. A list of inferences. Making inferences involves deducing hidden rules or facts from the given relationships between variables. Inferences almost always follow from a combination of the rules or limiting structural factors within the game.

By following the above list and using the scenario and rules from the game on the previous page, we can produce the setup as follows:

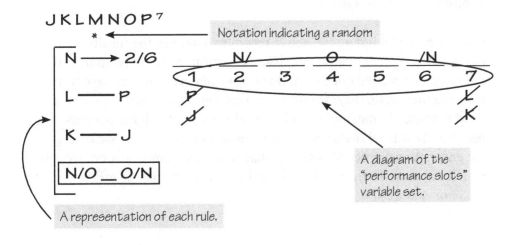

Remember to write legibly!

The above setup is linear in nature.

After making the
initial setup, do
not write on your
main diagram.

Once you have completed your game setup, you should *not* draw or otherwise write on your main diagram again. As you do each question, use the space *next* to the question to reproduce a miniature diagram with the basic structural features of your main diagram. You should *not* use your main diagram for the work of individual questions. For example, if a question introduces the condition that L sits in the third of seven chairs, draw the seven chair spaces next to the question, place L in the third space, make inferences, and then proceed with the question. Refer to your main setup for the details of the relationship between the variables. There are several important benefits that you receive from working next to the question: First, should you need to return to the question later, your work will be readily available and accessible; second, keeping the individual conditions of each question separate from the main setup reduces the possibility that you will mistake a local condition for a global rule; and third, you will be able to more clearly see which conditions produced which results.

Do the work for
each question
next to that
question.

As you complete each question, it is absolutely essential that you *not* erase your previous work. Each question that you complete adds to your repository of game knowledge, and that knowledge can be invaluable when answering other questions. For example, suppose the first question in a game produces a scenario where A is in the first position. Then, the second question asks for a complete and accurate listing of the positions A can occupy. Based on the first question, A can clearly be in the first position, and therefore you can eliminate any answer in the second question which does not contain the first position as a possibility. Thus, the work you do in *some* questions can be used to help answer other questions. This is true as long as the work you are referencing conforms to the conditions in the question you are currently answering. For example, if the third question in the same game states, "If A is in the third position, which one of the following can be true?" then you cannot use the information from the first question to help answer the third question because A was in the first position in the first question, and thus does not fit the condition imposed in the third question.

Do not erase
unless you make a
mistake.

The work done on
some questions
can be used to
help solve other
questions.

For students who ignore the above recommendations, the results are often quite negative: confusion, disorganization, constant rereading of the rules, and missed questions. Some students say that they save time by using their main diagram for each question. While they may save a short amount of time, the overall costs always outweigh the benefits, particularly since those same students have a tendency to erase during the game. As we proceed with our analysis of the games section, we will revisit this topic from time to time and ultimately prove the efficacy of our recommendations.

The Questions

Once you have completed your diagram and made inferences, you will be ready to answer the questions. Keep in mind that each question has exactly the same value and that there is no penalty for guessing. Thus, if you cannot complete the section you should guess on the questions that remain. If you cannot complete an individual question, do not spend an undue amount of time on the question. Instead, move on and complete the other questions.

Games questions are either global or local. Global questions ask about information derived only from the initial rules, such as "Who can finish first?" or "Which one of the following must be true?" Use the rules and your main diagram to answer global questions. Local questions generally begin with the words "if," "when," or "suppose," and occur when the question imposes a new condition in addition to the initial rules, such as "If Laura sits in the third chair, which one of the following must be true?" The additional conditions imposed by local questions apply to that question only and do not apply to any of the other questions. It is essential that you focus on the implications of the new conditions. Ask yourself how this condition affects the variables and the existing rules. For local questions, reproduce a mini-setup next to the question, apply the local condition, and proceed.

Within the global/local designation all questions ultimately ask for one of four things: what must be true, what is not necessarily true, what could be true, and what cannot be true. All questions are a variation of one of these four basic ideas. At all times, you must be aware of the exact nature of the question you are being asked, especially when "except" questions appear. If you discover you miss questions because you overlook terms like "false" or "except" when reading, take a moment at the beginning and circle key words in each question, such as "must," "could," etc.

The key to quickly answering questions is to identify with the rules and inferences in a game. This involves both properly diagramming the rules and simple memorization. If you often find yourself rereading the rules during a game, you are failing to identify with the rules. Do not forget to constantly apply your inferences to each question!

Guessing strategy is discussed in our Free LSAT Help area at powerscore.com

Local questions almost always require you to produce a "mini-setup" next to the question.

If you frequently misread questions, circle or underline the key part of each question before you begin the game. You will not forget about a word like "except" if you have it underlined!

The key to optimal performance on Logic Games is to be focused and organized. This involves a number of factors:

1. Play to your strengths and away from your weaknesses

You are not required to do the games in the order presented on the test, and you should not expect that the test makers will present the games in the best order for you. Students who expect to have difficulty on the games section should attack the games in order of their personal preferences and strengths and weaknesses. You can implement this strategy by quickly previewing each of the four games as you start the section. By doing so you can then select a game that you feel is the best fit for your strengths.

2. Create a strong setup for the game

Often, the key to powerful games performance is to create a good setup. At least 80% of the games on the LSAT are "setup games" wherein the quality of your setup dictates whether or not you are successful in answering the questions.

3. Look to make inferences

There are always inferences in a game, and the test makers expect you to make at least a few of them. Always check the rules and your setup with an eye towards finding inferences, and then use those inferences relentlessly to attack the questions.

4. Be smart during the game

If necessary, skip over time-consuming questions and return to them later. Remember that it is sometimes advisable to do the questions out of order. For example, if the first question in a game asks you for a complete and accurate list of the positions "C" could occupy, because of time considerations it would be advisable to skip that question and complete the remaining questions. Then you could return to the first question and use the knowledge you gained from the other questions to quickly and easily answer the first question.

Although test takers have found the first game on many LSATs to be the easiest, there is no set order of difficulty, and you cannot predict where the easiest or hardest game will appear. On some tests the first game has been the hardest and the last game has been the easiest. That said, for the majority of LSATs, the hardest game usually appears second or third, and the easiest game usually appears first.

5. Do not be intimidated by size

A lengthy game scenario and a large number of initial rules do not necessarily equal greater difficulty. Some of the longest games are easy because they contain so many restrictions and limitations.

6. Keep an awareness of time

As stated previously, you have approximately eight minutes and forty-five seconds to complete each game and bubble in your answers. Use a timer during the LSAT so you always know how much time remains, and do not let one game or question consume so much time that you suffer later on.

7. Maintain a positive attitude and stay focused

Above all, you must attack each game with a positive and energetic attitude. The games themselves are often challenging yet fun, and students who actively involve themselves in the games generally perform better overall.

Thus far we have provided a very basic overview of the Logic Games section; subsequent chapters present individual games classified according to the *PowerScore LSAT Logic Games Bible* system.

Memorize these points! They are basic principles you must know in order to perform powerfully.

If you complete all four games, you have 8 minutes and 45 seconds to complete each game, inclusive of answer transferring. If you do only three games, you have 11 minutes and 40 seconds to complete each game. If you do just two games, you have 17 minutes and 30 seconds to complete each game.

You can do the games out of order and according to your strengths and weaknesses.

There are three parts to every Logic Game: the scenario, the rules, and the questions.

Always read the scenario and rules once through before you begin diagramming.

Fix the rules in your mind.

Make a main diagram for each game. Include the following:

> List the variables and their exact total number
> Identify randoms
> Diagram the variable sets
> Diagram the rules
> Make inferences
> Identify the powerful rules and variables

Write neatly.

You can do the questions out of order if it saves time or is more efficient.

For local questions, do your work next to the question whenever possible.

Always look to use your inferences when answering questions.

Do not erase unless you have made a mistake.

Do not forget that work from one question might be useful on other questions.

Maintain a positive attitude, stay focused, and try to enjoy yourself.

Logic Games Classifications Explained

In the following chapters, the Logic Games from PrepTests 1 through 20 are presented in groups by classification type. The classification system we use is comprehensive, and is explained in detail in the *PowerScore LSAT Logic Games Bible*. The following is a brief description of each classification type.

Basic Linear Games

Linearity involves the fixed positioning and ordering of variables. Basic Linear Games feature just two variable sets, one of which is chosen as the "base" and is diagrammed in a straight line, either horizontally or vertically. The other variable set is placed into slots above or next to the base.

Here is an example Basic Linear game scenario, from earlier in this chapter:

> Seven comics—Janet, Khan, Leticia, Ming, Neville, Olivia, and Paul—will be scheduled to perform in the finals of a comedy competition. During the evening of the competition, each comic, performing alone, will give exactly one performance.

The Importance of Numbers: Balanced vs. Unbalanced Games

A "Balanced" game (such as the one above) occurs when the number of supplied variables equals the number of available slots, resulting in a one-to-one numerical relationship of variables to slots. As you might expect, not every Linear game features a Balanced scenario, and since Unbalanced games are generally more difficult than Balanced games, it is to your advantage to be able to recognize what type of numerical situation you are facing.

There are two types of Unbalanced Linear games: Underfunded and Overloaded. Underfunded games feature a fewer number of variables than available slots, for example, seven passengers assigned to nine seats on a plane. Overloaded games feature a greater number of variables than available slots; for example, eight piano lessons to be taught over five days. Overloaded scenarios often produce the most difficult Linear games.

Each game type is explained here in basic terms. For a comprehensive discussion of each classification, and how to best solve each type, we recommend that you pick up a copy of the PowerScore LSAT Logic Games Bible.

Advanced Linear Games

Advanced Linear Games are the same as Basic Linear Games, but instead of two variable sets they feature three to five variable sets.

Here is a sample Advanced Linear game scenario:

> Exactly six runners—P, Q, R, S, T, and U—compete in a marathon. Each runner finishes the race, and no two runners finish at the same time. The information that follows is all that is known about the six runners:
> > Each runner is either an amateur or a professional, but not both.
> > Four of the runners are female and two are male.

In most other respects Advanced Linear games are similar to Basic Linear games, and issues of Balance also occur in Advanced Linear games.

Grouping Games

Grouping games require you to analyze the variables in terms of which ones can and cannot be together. In grouping games the emphasis on ordering—the basis of linear games—is typically not present. Consider the following example:

> A four-person research group is selected from seven candidates—H, J, K, L, M, O, and R. The group is selected according to the following restrictions:
> > If J is selected, then R is selected.
> > If R is selected, then H is not selected.

In this game the concept of order or linearity does not appear; instead, the focus is on placing the variables into a workable group.

Unified Grouping Theory™

Games that involve grouping can generally be broken down into one of the following two categories:

Defined: In these games the exact number of variables to be selected is given in the rules.

Undefined: It is uncertain exactly how many variables are to be selected for the game, or there are several different possibilities. For example, a committee of at least three members is formed from among ten candidates.

Partially Defined™: There is a minimum and/or maximum number of variables to be selected in these games, but the *exact* number of variables selected in the game cannot be determined.

In addition, all Defined games (and some Undefined games) can be broken into the following subclassifications:

Balanced: The number of variables to be selected is equal to the overall number of available spaces. For example, eight students are divided into two four-person study groups.

Unbalanced: The number of variables to be selected is not equal to the overall number of available spaces. Unbalanced games are either Overloaded or Underfunded:

Overloaded: There are extra candidates for the available spaces. For example, nine candidates for a five-person research panel.

Underfunded: There are not enough candidates for the available spaces. This lack is almost always solved by reusing one or more of the candidates. For example, seven products to be advertised over a period of nine weeks.

Grouping/Linear Combination Games

Grouping and linearity are the two fundamental principles test makers use to form the Logic Games section, and typically at least 75% of the games in each section feature at least one of these ideas. It is not surprising, therefore, to see a number of games that combine these ideas.

Typically, in Grouping/Linear combination games an Unbalanced: Overloaded set of variables must be narrowed down and then the remaining variables must be placed into a diagram that has a linear element. For example, consider the following:

> A theater director must select exactly seven of nine plays to be presented over seven consecutive months, January through July.

Pure Sequencing Games

Pure Sequencing games involve the ranking or ordering of variables. The key to recognizing a pure sequencing game is that the relationships between the variables are relative and not precisely fixed.

Here is an example Sequencing game scenario:

> Each of seven runners—Q, R, S, T, U, W, and Y—runs a race and finishes in a different position: from first through seventh (from fastest to slowest). The finishing positions are consistent with the following conditions:
> R is faster than S.
> U is slower than T.
> Q is faster than R and T.

Pattern Games

Pattern games are a variation of Linear games. In a Pattern game, the rules govern the general action of all variables, as opposed to the specific variable governance found in standard Linear games. Thus, instead of rules defining the specific placement of a variable, such as "P must speak third," Pattern game rules generally affect the action of all variables, as in "Each candidate must speak either first or second at at least one of the meetings." Consider the following game scenario:

> A traveling salesman makes five trips around a circle of five cities—F, G, H, J, and K—stopping at exactly three of the cities on each trip. The train must conform to the following conditions:
>> The salesman stops at any given city on exactly three trips, but not on three consecutive trips.
>> The salesman stops at any given city at least once in any two consecutive trips.

Circular Linearity

Circular Linearity games consist of a fixed number of variables assigned to spaces distributed around a circle. Usually the scenario involves people sitting around a table. Essentially these games are Linear games wrapped around a circular diagram (hence the name), and linearity is still the controlling principle. Consider the following example:

> Eight individuals sit around a circular conference table with eight chairs. At most one individual sits in each chair.

Mapping Games

All Logic Games can be classified as numerical or non-numerical. The vast majority of games are numerical in nature, where numbers play an important role in the game solution (Linear, Grouping, Pattern, etc.). The only non-numerical game type is Mapping, and even within Mapping games, some contain enough grouping as to be numerical.

There are three types of Mapping games:

1. Spatial Relations. The rules in these games do not fix the physical relationships among the variables. For example, a game involving shelter sites in a park simply states that certain shelters are one day's hike from each other. Using this information allows the test taker to ascertain the relationship among the variables, but not their exact positions. Whether a variable is north or south of another variable is generally meaningless in games of this type. The best approach for

these games is to diagram the relationships with arrows or lines.

2. <u>Directional</u>. These games involve a fixed point, and all other variables are placed North, East, South, and West of that point. For example, one game fixes City Hall as the center of a town and then proceeds to place all variables directionally by referencing City Hall. The best approach to this type of game is to use the fixed center point and draw each of the four quadrants (NE, SE, SW, and NW) around the center point.

Although Directional games appeared several times in the 1980s, there has not been a pure Directional game since then. However, some games have featured directional elements, such as the Park Bench game in this book from the October 1992 LSAT.

3. <u>Supplied Diagram</u>. In these games the makers of the test supply a diagram intended to represent the relationship of the variables. Always use the diagram!

Advanced Features and Techniques: Numerical Distribution Games and Limited Solution Set Games

Games in this section are of various types, but feature either a Numerical Distribution, a limiting element, or both.

Numerical Distributions

A Numerical Distribution allocates one set of variables among another set of variables. Since the distribution controls the placement of variables, the distribution is a basic, but critical, element in the game.

A Numerical Distribution is a game feature, not a separate game type.

Limited Solution Set Games

Certain Logic Games are so restricted that only a limited number of solutions conform to the rules. In these games the best approach is to diagram each possibility before attacking the questions. With all of the possibilities in hand, the questions are easy.

Limited Solution Sets are a feature that appear in many different game types, including Grouping and Linear games, but there is no specific type of game that *always* uses this feature. Typically, the number of possibilities is constrained by some type of restriction or limitation that leads to just a few solutions.

Identify the Templates™

When a game is attacked by Identifying the Templates, the major possibility templates are diagrammed, but the exact possibilities within each template are not fully displayed.

Identify the Possibilities™

Identify the Possibilities is an extension of Identify the Templates. Instead of creating basic templates to capture the general direction of the game, each possibility is written out. This usually takes more time during the setup, but since it results in perfect information the questions can be answered incredibly fast.

The difference between showing templates and possibilities is one of degree. Identifying the Templates exposes the major directions of the game; Identifying the Possibilities explores those directions in detail. Because Identifying the Templates is less detailed, it tends to take less time to apply. On the contrary, Identifying the Possibilities takes longer because it is more detailed.

Identify the Templates and Identify the Possibilities are not game types; rather, they are techniques for attacking certain games.

Chapter Two:
Basic Linear Games

Chapter Two: Basic Linear Games

Game #1: October 1991 Questions 6-12

An apartment building has five floors. Each floor has either one or two apartments. There are exactly eight apartments in the building. The residents of the building are J, K, L, M, N, O, P, and Q, who each live in a different apartment.

    J lives on a floor with two apartments.
    K lives on the floor directly above P.
    The second floor is made up of only one apartment.
    M and N live on the same floor.
    O does not live on the same floor as Q.
    L lives in the only apartment on her floor.
    Q does not live on the first or second floor.

6.   Which one of the following must be true?

    (A)   Q lives on the third floor.
    (B)   Q lives on the fifth floor.
    (C)   L does not live on the fourth floor.
    (D)   N does not live on the second floor.
    (E)   J lives on the first floor.

7.   Which one of the following CANNOT be true?

    (A)   K lives on the second floor.
    (B)   M lives on the first floor.
    (C)   N lives on the fourth floor.
    (D)   O lives on the third floor.
    (E)   P lives on the fifth floor.

8.   If J lives on the fourth floor and K lives on the fifth floor, which one of the following can be true?

    (A)   O lives on the first floor.
    (B)   Q lives on the fourth floor.
    (C)   N lives on the fifth floor.
    (D)   L lives on the fourth floor.
    (E)   P lives on the third floor.

9.   If O lives on the second floor, which one of the following CANNOT be true?

    (A)   K lives on the fourth floor.
    (B)   K lives on the fifth floor.
    (C)   L lives on the first floor.
    (D)   L lives on the third floor.
    (E)   L lives on the fourth floor.

10.   If M lives on the fourth floor, which one of the following must be false?

    (A)   O lives on the fifth floor.
    (B)   J lives on the first floor.
    (C)   L lives on the second floor.
    (D)   Q lives on the third floor.
    (E)   P lives on the first floor.

11.   Which one of the following must be true?

    (A)   If J lives on the fourth floor, then Q does not live on the fifth floor.
    (B)   If O lives on the second floor, then L does not live on the fourth floor.
    (C)   If N lives on the fourth floor, then K does not live on the second floor.
    (D)   If K lives on the third floor, then O does not live on the fifth floor.
    (E)   If P lives on the fourth floor, then M does not live on the third floor.

12.   If O lives on the fourth floor and P lives on the second floor, which one of the following must be true?

    (A)   L lives on the first floor.
    (B)   M lives on the third floor.
    (C)   Q lives on the third floor.
    (D)   N lives on the fifth floor.
    (E)   Q lives on the fifth floor.

Game #2: December 1991 Questions 8-13

There are exactly seven houses on a street. Each house is occupied by exactly one of seven families: the Kahns, Lowes, Muirs, Newmans, Owens, Piatts, Rutans. All the houses are on the same side of the street, which runs from west to east.

The Rutans do not live in the first or the last house on the street.
The Kahns live in the fourth house from the west end of the street.
The Muirs live next to the Kahns.
The Piatts live east of both the Kahns and the Muirs, but west of the Lowes.

8. Which one of the following families could live in the house that is the farthest east?

   (A)   the Kahns
   (B)   the Muirs
   (C)   the Newmans
   (D)   the Piatts
   (E)   the Rutans

9. Which one of the following families CANNOT live next to the Kahns?

   (A)   the Lowes
   (B)   the Newmans
   (C)   the Owens
   (D)   the Piatts
   (E)   the Rutans

10. If the Muirs live west of the Kahns, then the Rutans CANNOT live next to both

   (A)   the Kahns and the Piatts
   (B)   the Lowes and the Piatts
   (C)   the Muirs and the Piatts
   (D)   the Muirs and the Owens
   (E)   the Muirs and the Newmans

11. If the Newmans live immediately west of the Kahns, which one of the following statements must be false?

   (A)   The Owens live next to the Newmans.
   (B)   The Owens live next to the Rutans.
   (C)   The Piatts live next to the Lowes.
   (D)   The Piatts live next to the Muirs.
   (E)   The Rutans live next to the Newmans.

12. If the Owens live east of the Muirs, which one of the following statements must be true?

   (A)   The Kahns live east of the Muirs.
   (B)   The Kahns live west of the Rutans.
   (C)   The Owens live west of the Lowes.
   (D)   The Owens live east of the Piatts.
   (E)   The Owens live west of the Piatts.

13. If the Owens live east of the Kahns, which one of the following pairs of families must live next to each other?

   (A)   the Kahns and the Piatts
   (B)   the Lowes and the Owens
   (C)   the Muirs and the Newmans
   (D)   the Newmans and the Rutans
   (E)   the Owens and the Piatts

Game #3: June 1992 Questions 1-6

John receives one grade for each of the following six
courses: economics, geology, history, Italian, physics,
and Russian. From highest to lowest, the possible
grades are A, B, C, D, and E. E is the only failing grade.
Two letter grades are consecutive if and only if they are
adjacent in the alphabet.

    John's grades in geology and physics are
     consecutive.
    His grades in Italian and Russian are consecutive.
    He receives a higher grade in economics than in
     history.
    He receives a higher grade in geology than in
     physics.

1. If John receives the same grade in economics and
    Italian, and if he fails Russian, which one of the
    following must be true?

    (A) John's geology grade is a B.
    (B) John's history grade is a D.
    (C) John's history grade is an E.
    (D) John's physics grade is a B.
    (E) John's physics grade is a C.

2. If John passes all his courses and receives a higher
    grade in geology than in either language, which
    one of the following must be true?

    (A) He receives exactly one A.
    (B) He receives exactly one B.
    (C) He receives exactly two Bs.
    (D) He receives at least one B and at least one C.
    (E) He receives at least one C and at least one D.

3. If John receives a higher grade in physics than
    in economics and receives a higher grade in
    economics than in either language, which one of
    the following allows all six of his grades to be
    determined?

    (A) His grade in history is D.
    (B) His grade in Italian is D.
    (C) His grades in history and Italian are
         identical.
    (D) His grades in history and Russian are
         identical.
    (E) His grade in history is higher than his grade
         in Russian.

4. If John receives a higher grade in physics than in
    economics and receives a higher grade in history
    than in Italian, exactly how many of his grades can
    be determined?

    (A) 2
    (B) 3
    (C) 4
    (D) 5
    (E) 6

5. Assume that John's grade in physics is higher than
    his grade in Italian and consecutive with it and that
    his grades in Russian and physics differ. Which one
    of the following must be true?

    (A) John receives both an A and a B.
    (B) John receives both an A and a C.
    (C) John receives both a B and a D.
    (D) John receives both a B and an E.
    (E) John receives both a D and an E.

6. Assume that John receives a lower grade in
    economics than in physics. He must have failed at
    least one course if which one of the following is
    also true?

    (A) He receives a lower grade in Italian than in
         economics.
    (B) He receives a lower grade in Italian than in
         physics.
    (C) He receives a lower grade in physics than in
         Italian.
    (D) He receives a lower grade in Russian than in
         economics.
    (E) He receives a lower grade in Russian than in
         history.

Game #4: February 1993 Questions 1-7

Seven consecutive time slots for a broadcast, numbered in chronological order 1 through 7, will be filled by six song tapes—G, H, L, O, P, S—and exactly one news tape. Each tape is to be assigned to a different time slot, and no tape is longer than any other tape. The broadcast is subject to the following restrictions:

L must be played immediately before O.

The news tape must be played at some time after L. There must be exactly two time slots between G and P, regardless of whether G comes before P or whether G comes after P.

1. If G is played second, which one of the following tapes must be played third?

   (A)   the news
   (B)   H
   (C)   L
   (D)   O
   (E)   S

2. The news tape can be played in any one of the following time slots EXCEPT the

   (A)   second
   (B)   third
   (C)   fourth
   (D)   fifth
   (E)   sixth

3. If H and S are to be scheduled as far from each other as possible, then the first, the second, and the third time slots could be filled, respectively, by

   (A)   G, H, and L
   (B)   S, G, and the news
   (C)   H, G, and L
   (D)   H, L, and O
   (E)   L, O, and S

4. If P is played fifth, L must be played

   (A)   first
   (B)   second
   (C)   third
   (D)   fourth
   (E)   sixth

5. What is the maximum number of tapes that can separate S from the news?

   (A)   1
   (B)   2
   (C)   3
   (D)   4
   (E)   5

6. Which one of the following is the latest time slot in which L can be played?

   (A)   the third
   (B)   the fourth
   (C)   the fifth
   (D)   the sixth
   (E)   the seventh

7. The time slot in which O must be played is completely determined if G is assigned to which one of the following time slots?

   (A)   the first
   (B)   the third
   (C)   the fourth
   (D)   the fifth
   (E)   the sixth

Game #5: June 1993 Questions 1-5

A gymnastics instructor is planning a weekly schedule, Monday through Friday, of individual coaching sessions for each of six students—H, I, K, O, U, and Z. The instructor will coach exactly one student each day, except for one day when the instructor will coach two students in separate but consecutive sessions. The following restrictions apply:

H's session must take place at some time before Z's session.

I's session is on Thursday.

K's session is always scheduled for the day immediately before or the day immediately after the day for which O's session is scheduled.

Neither Monday nor Wednesday can be a day for which two students are scheduled.

1. Which one of the following is a pair of students whose sessions can both be scheduled for Tuesday, not necessarily in the order given?

   (A) H and U
   (B) H and Z
   (C) K and O
   (D) O and U
   (E) U and Z

2. If K's session is scheduled for Tuesday, then which one of the following is the earliest day for which Z's session can be scheduled?

   (A) Monday
   (B) Tuesday
   (C) Wednesday
   (D) Thursday
   (E) Friday

3. Which one of the following must be true?

   (A) If U's session is scheduled for Monday, H's session is scheduled for Tuesday.
   (B) If U's session is scheduled for Tuesday, O's session is scheduled for Wednesday.
   (C) If U's session is scheduled for Wednesday, Z's session is scheduled for Tuesday.
   (D) If U's session is scheduled for Thursday, Z's session is scheduled for Friday.
   (E) If U's session is scheduled for Friday, Z's session is scheduled for Thursday.

4. Scheduling Z's session for which one of the following days determines the day for which U's session must be scheduled?

   (A) Monday
   (B) Tuesday
   (C) Wednesday
   (D) Thursday
   (E) Friday

5. If H's session is scheduled as the next session after U's session, which one of the following could be true about H's session and U's session?

   (A) U's session is scheduled for Monday, and H's session is scheduled for Tuesday.
   (B) U's session is scheduled for Thursday, and H's session is scheduled for Friday.
   (C) They are both scheduled for Tuesday.
   (D) They are both scheduled for Thursday.
   (E) They are both scheduled for Friday.

Game #6: December 1994 Questions 7-11

Five people—Harry, Iris, Kate, Nancy, and Victor—are to be scheduled as contestants on a television show, one contestant per day, for five consecutive days from Monday through Friday. The following restrictions governing the scheduling of contestants must be observed:

> Nancy is not scheduled for Monday.
> If Harry is scheduled for Monday, Nancy is scheduled for Friday.
> If Nancy is scheduled for Tuesday, Iris is scheduled for Monday.
> Kate is scheduled for the next day after the day for which Victor is scheduled.

7. Victor can be scheduled for any day EXCEPT

   (A) Monday
   (B) Tuesday
   (C) Wednesday
   (D) Thursday
   (E) Friday

8. If Iris is scheduled for the next day after Harry, which one of the following lists all those days any one of which could be the day for which Harry is scheduled?

   (A) Monday, Tuesday
   (B) Monday, Wednesday
   (C) Monday, Thursday
   (D) Monday, Tuesday, Wednesday
   (E) Monday, Wednesday, Thursday

9. If Kate is scheduled for Wednesday, which one of the following could be true?

   (A) Iris is scheduled for Friday.
   (B) Nancy is scheduled for Tuesday.
   (C) Nancy is scheduled for an earlier day than the day for which Harry is scheduled.
   (D) Nancy is scheduled for an earlier day than the day for which Iris is scheduled.
   (E) Nancy is scheduled for an earlier day than the day for which Kate is scheduled.

10. If Kate is scheduled for Friday, which one of the following must be true?

    (A) Harry is scheduled for Tuesday.
    (B) Harry is scheduled for Wednesday.
    (C) Iris is scheduled for Monday.
    (D) Iris is scheduled for Wednesday.
    (E) Nancy is scheduled for Wednesday.

11. If Iris is scheduled for Wednesday, which one of the following must be true?

    (A) Harry is scheduled for an earlier day than the day for which Nancy is scheduled.
    (B) Harry is scheduled for an earlier day than the day for which Kate is scheduled.
    (C) Kate is scheduled for an earlier day than the day for which Harry is scheduled.
    (D) Nancy is scheduled for an earlier day than the day for which Kate is scheduled.
    (E) Nancy is scheduled for an earlier day than the day for which Iris is scheduled.

Game #7: June 1995 Questions 1-6

A professor will listen to exactly one speech from each of six students—H, J, K, R, S, and T. The six speeches will be delivered one at a time, consecutively, according to the following conditions:

The speeches delivered by H, J, and K, no matter what their order relative to each other, cannot form a sequence of three consecutive speeches.

The speeches delivered by R, S, and T, no matter what their order relative to each other, cannot form a sequence of three consecutive speeches.

H's speech must be earlier than S's speech.

J's speech can be neither first nor sixth.

T's speech can be neither immediately before nor immediately after J's speech.

1. Which one of the following could be the order, from first to last, in which the students deliver their speeches?

   (A)   H, J, R, S, T, K
   (B)   H, R, T, K, S, J
   (C)   K, J, T, H, S, R
   (D)   R, J, K, T, H, S
   (E)   T, R, J, S, K, H

2. If T delivers the third speech, which one of the following must be true?

   (A)   H delivers the first speech.
   (B)   J delivers the fifth speech.
   (C)   K delivers the fourth speech.
   (D)   R delivers the sixth speech.
   (E)   S delivers the fourth speech.

3. If S delivers the third speech and T delivers the fourth speech, then which one of the following must be true?

   (A)   H delivers the second speech.
   (B)   J delivers the fifth speech.
   (C)   K delivers the fifth speech.
   (D)   K delivers the first speech.
   (E)   R delivers the first speech.

4. If K delivers the first speech and H delivers the fifth speech, which one of the following must be true?

   (A)   R delivers the third speech.
   (B)   T delivers the fourth speech.
   (C)   J's speech is immediately before H's speech.
   (D)   K's speech is immediately before T's speech.
   (E)   R's speech is immediately before J's speech.

5. If R's speech is immediately after S's speech and immediately before K's speech, then which one of the following could be true?

   (A)   H's speech is immediately before S's speech.
   (B)   H's speech is immediately before T's speech.
   (C)   K's speech is immediately before J's speech.
   (D)   K's speech is immediately before T's speech.
   (E)   T's speech is immediately before S's speech.

6. If K delivers the third speech, any of the following could be the student who makes the fourth speech EXCEPT

   (A)   H
   (B)   J
   (C)   R
   (D)   S
   (E)   T

Game #8: December 1995 Questions 1-5

On Wednesday a physician will have exactly one appointment with seven patients—P, Q, R, S, T, U, W—one patient per appointment. The schedule of appointments, chronologically numbered 1 through 7, must meet the following conditions:

   Q's appointment is at some time before W's appointment.
   U's appointment is at some time before P's appointment.
   Either R or T has appointment 3.
   S's appointment is either the appointment immediately before or the appointment immediately after R's appointment.

1. Which one of the following is an acceptable schedule of appointments in order from 1 to 7?

   (A)   Q, S, R, P, W, U, T
   (B)   Q, U, W, S, R, T, P
   (C)   S, Q, R, T, W, U, P
   (D)   T, U, R, S, W, P, Q
   (E)   U, Q, T, P, R, S, W

2. If W has appointment 2 and P has appointment 5, then which one of the following must be true?

   (A)   R has appointment 6.
   (B)   S has appointment 4.
   (C)   S has appointment 7.
   (D)   U has appointment 1.
   (E)   U has appointment 4.

3. If U's appointment is immediately after T's appointment and immediately before R's appointment, then which one of the following must be true

   (A)   Q's appointment is at some time before P's appointment.
   (B)   S's appointment is at some time before P's appointment.
   (C)   S's appointment is immediately before Q's appointment.
   (D)   W's appointment is immediately before P's appointment.
   (E)   W's appointment is at some time before S's appointment.

4. If P's appointment is immediately before S's appointment, then each of the following could be true EXCEPT:

   (A)   R's appointment is immediately before W's appointment.
   (B)   T's appointment is immediately before Q's appointment.
   (C)   U's appointment is immediately before P's appointment.
   (D)   U's appointment is immediately before Q's appointment.
   (E)   W's appointment is immediately before T's appointment.

5. If T's appointment is immediately after P's appointment and immediately before W's appointment, then which one of the following must be true?

   (A)   W's appointment is at some time before R's appointment.
   (B)   U's appointment is at some time before R's appointment.
   (C)   S's appointment is at some time before U's appointment.
   (D)   R's appointment is at some time before P's appointment.
   (E)   Q's appointment is at some time before S's appointment.

Game #9: June 1996 Questions 1-7

During a period of six consecutive days—day 1 through day 6—each of exactly six factories—F, G, H, J, Q, and R—will be inspected. During this period, each of the factories will be inspected exactly once, one factory per day. The schedule for the inspections must conform to the following conditions:

F is inspected on either day 1 or day 6.

J is inspected on an earlier day than Q is inspected.

Q is inspected on the day immediately before R is inspected.

If G is inspected on day 3, Q is inspected on day 5.

1. Which one of the following could be a list of the factories in the order of their scheduled inspections, from day 1 through day 6?

    (A)   F, Q, R, H, J, G
    (B)   G, H, J, Q, R, F
    (C)   G, J, Q, H, R, F
    (D)   G, J, Q, R, F, H
    (E)   J, H, G, Q, R, F

2. Which one of the following must be false?

    (A)   The inspection of G is scheduled for day 4.
    (B)   The inspection of H is scheduled for day 6.
    (C)   The inspection of J is scheduled for day 4.
    (D)   The inspection of Q is scheduled for day 3.
    (E)   The inspection of R is scheduled for day 2.

3. The inspection of which one of the following CANNOT be scheduled for day 5?

    (A)   G
    (B)   H
    (C)   J
    (D)   Q
    (E)   R

4. The inspections scheduled for day 3 and day 5, respectively, could be those of

    (A)   G and H
    (B)   G and R
    (C)   H and G
    (D)   R and J
    (E)   R and H

5. If the inspection of R is scheduled for the day immediately before the inspection of F, which one of the following must be true about the schedule?

    (A)   The inspection of either G or H is scheduled for day 1.
    (B)   The inspection of either G or J is scheduled for day 1.
    (C)   The inspection of either G or J is scheduled for day 2.
    (D)   The inspection of either H or J is scheduled for day 3.
    (E)   The inspection of either H or J is scheduled for day 4.

6. If the inspections of G and of H are scheduled, not necessarily in that order, for days as far apart as possible, which one of the following is a complete and accurate list of the factories any one of which could be scheduled for inspection for day 1?

    (A)   F, J
    (B)   G, H
    (C)   G, H, J
    (D)   F, G, H
    (E)   F, G, H, J

7. If the inspection of G is scheduled for the day immediately before the inspection of Q, which one of the following could be true?

    (A)   The inspection of G is scheduled for day 5.
    (B)   The inspection of H is scheduled for day 6.
    (C)   The inspection of J is scheduled for day 2.
    (D)   The inspection of Q is scheduled for day 4.
    (E)   The inspection of R is scheduled for day 3.

Chapter Three:
Advanced Linear Games

Chapter Three: Advanced Linear Games

A small software firm has four offices, numbered 1, 2, 3, and 4. Each of its offices has exactly one computer and exactly one printer. Each of these eight machines was bought in either 1987, 1988, or 1989. The eight machines were bought in a manner consistent with the following conditions:

The computer in each office was bought either in an earlier year than or in the same year as the printer in that office.

The computer in office 2 and the printer in office 1 were bought in the same year.

The computer in office 3 and the printer in office 4 were bought in the same year.

The computer in office 2 and the computer in office 3 were bought in different years.

The computer in office 1 and the printer in office 3 were bought in 1988.

8. If the computer in office 3 was bought in an earlier year than the printer in office 3 was, then which one of the following statements could be true?

    (A)   The computer in office 2 was bought in 1987.
    (B)   The computer in office 2 was bought in 1988.
    (C)   The computer in office 4 was bought in 1988.
    (D)   The printer in office 4 was bought in 1988.
    (E)   The printer in office 4 was bought in 1989.

9. Which one of the following statements could be true?

    (A)   The printer in office 1 was bought in 1987.
    (B)   The computer in office 2 was bought in 1987.
    (C)   The computer in office 3 was bought in 1989.
    (D)   The printer in office 4 was bought in 1988.
    (E)   The printer in office 4 was bought in 1989.

10. If as few of the eight machines as possible were bought in 1987, then what is the exact number of machines that were bought in 1987?

    (A)   0
    (B)   1
    (C)   2
    (D)   3
    (E)   4

11. If the computer in office 4 was bought in 1988, then which one of the following statements must be true?

    (A)   The printer in office 1 was bought in 1988.
    (B)   The printer in office 1 was bought in 1989.
    (C)   The computer in office 2 was bought in 1988.
    (D)   The computer in office 3 was bought in 1987.
    (E)   The printer in office 4 was bought in 1989.

12. If the computer in office 3 was bought in 1988, then which one of the following statements could be true?

    (A)   The printer in office 1 was bought in 1988.
    (B)   The computer in office 2 was bought in 1987.
    (C)   The printer in office 2 was bought in 1988.
    (D)   The computer in office 4 was bought in 1987.
    (E)   The printer in office 4 was bought in 1989.

13. Suppose that the computer in office 2 and the computer in office 3 had been bought in the same year as each other. If all of the other conditions remained the same, then which one of the following machines could have been bought in 1989?

    (A)   the printer in office 1
    (B)   the computer in office 2
    (C)   the printer in office 2
    (D)   the computer in office 4
    (E)   the printer in office 4

A railway company has exactly three lines: line 1, line 2, and line 3. The company prints three sets of tickets for January and three sets of tickets for February: one set for each of its lines for each of the two months. The company's tickets are printed in a manner consistent with the following conditions:

    Each of the six sets of tickets is exactly one of the following colors: green, purple, red, yellow.

    For each line, the January tickets are a different color than the February tickets.

    For each month, tickets for different lines are in different colors.

    Exactly one set of January tickets is red.

    For line 3, either the January tickets or the February tickets, but not both, are green.

    The January tickets for line 2 are purple.

    No February tickets are purple.

19. If the line 3 tickets for January are red, then which one of the following statements must be true?

  (A) The line 1 tickets for January are green.
  (B) The line 1 tickets for January are yellow.
  (C) The line 1 tickets for February are red.
  (D) The line 2 tickets for February are yellow.
  (E) The line 3 tickets for February are green.

20. If one set of the line 2 tickets is green, then which one of the following statements must be true?

  (A) The line 1 tickets for January are red.
  (B) The line 3 tickets for January are red.
  (C) The line 1 tickets for February are red.
  (D) The line 3 tickets for February are green.
  (E) The line 3 tickets for February are yellow.

21. Which one of the following statements could be true?

  (A) No January ticket is green.
  (B) No February ticket is green.
  (C) Only line 2 tickets are red.
  (D) One set of January tickets is green and one set of January tickets is yellow.
  (E) The line 2 tickets for January are the same color as the line 1 tickets for February.

22. Which one of the following statements could be true?

  (A) Both the line 1 tickets for January and the line 2 tickets for February are green.
  (B) Both the line 1 tickets for January and the line 2 tickets for February are yellow.
  (C) Both the line 1 tickets for January and the line 3 tickets for February are yellow.
  (D) The line 1 tickets for January are green, and the line 3 tickets for February are red.
  (E) The line 3 tickets for January are yellow, and the line 1 tickets for February are red.

23. If the line 3 tickets for February are yellow, then each of the following statements must be true EXCEPT:

  (A) One set of January tickets is green.
  (B) One set of line 1 tickets is red.
  (C) One set of line 2 tickets is red.
  (D) The tickets in two of the six sets are red.
  (E) The tickets in two of the six sets are yellow.

24. Suppose that none of the ticket sets are purple. If all of the other conditions remain the same, then which one of the following statements could be true?

  (A) None of the January tickets are green.
  (B) None of the February tickets are green.
  (C) None of the line 2 tickets are green.
  (D) No line 1 or line 2 tickets are yellow.
  (E) No line 2 or line 3 tickets are red.

ADVANCED LINEAR

Exactly six dogs—P, Q, R, S, T, and U—are entered in a dog show. The judge of the show awards exactly four ribbons, one for each of first, second, third, and fourth places, to four of the dogs. The information that follows is all that is available about the six dogs:

Each dog is either a greyhound or a labrador, but not both.

Two of the six dogs are female and four are male.

The judge awards ribbons to both female dogs, exactly one of which is a labrador.

Exactly one labrador wins a ribbon.

Dogs P and R place ahead of dog S, and dog S places ahead of dogs Q and T.

Dogs P and R are greyhounds.

Dogs S and U are labradors.

18. Which one of the following is a complete and accurate list of the dogs that can be greyhounds?

    (A) P, Q
    (B) P, R
    (C) P, Q, R
    (D) P, R, T
    (E) P, Q, R, T

19. Which one of the following statements CANNOT be true?

    (A) A female greyhound wins the second place ribbon.
    (B) A female labrador wins the second place ribbon.
    (C) A female labrador wins the third place ribbon.
    (D) A male greyhound wins the fourth place ribbon.
    (E) A female greyhound wins the fourth place ribbon.

20. Which one of the following dogs must be male?

    (A) dog P
    (B) dog R
    (C) dog S
    (D) dog T
    (E) dog U

21. Which one of the following statements can be false?

    (A) Dog P places ahead of dog R.
    (B) Dog P places ahead of dog T.
    (C) Dog R places ahead of dog U.
    (D) Dog R places ahead of dog T.
    (E) Dog S places ahead of dog U.

22. If dog Q is female, which one of the following statements can be false?

    (A) Dog P is male.
    (B) Dog R is male.
    (C) Dog Q wins the fourth place ribbon.
    (D) Dog Q is a greyhound.
    (E) Dog T is a greyhound.

23. If dog T wins the fourth place ribbon, then which one of the following statements must be true?

    (A) Dog P is male.
    (B) Dog Q is male.
    (C) Dog T is male.
    (D) Dog Q is a labrador.
    (E) Dog T is a labrador.

24. Which one of the following statements could be true?

    (A) Dog P does not win a ribbon.
    (B) Dog R does not win a ribbon.
    (C) Dog S does not win a ribbon.
    (D) Dog T wins a ribbon.
    (E) Dog U wins a ribbon.

At an automobile exhibition, cars are displayed on each floor of a three-floor building. On each floor the cars are either all family cars or all sports cars, either all new or all used, and either all production models or all research models. The following conditions apply to this exhibition:

> If the exhibition includes both family cars and sports cars, then each family car is displayed on a lower-numbered floor than any sports car.
> The exhibition includes no used research models.
> The exhibition includes no research models that are sports cars.
> There are new cars on floor 1.
> There are used cars on floor 3.

14. If there are sports cars on exactly two floors, then which one of the following statements could be true?

    (A) There are research models on floor 1.
    (B) There are sports cars on floor 1.
    (C) There are family cars on floor 2.
    (D) There are research models on floor 2.
    (E) There are family cars on floor 3.

15. Which one of the following statements could be true?

    (A) The exhibition includes new research model sports cars.
    (B) The exhibition includes used research model family cars.
    (C) The exhibition includes used research model sports cars.
    (D) There are research models on exactly one floor.
    (E) There are research models on all three floors.

16. Which one of the following statements must be true?

    (A) There are production models on floor 1.
    (B) There are research models on floor 1.
    (C) There are production models on floor 2.
    (D) There are production models on floor 3.
    (E) There are research models on floor 3.

17. If there are research models on exactly two floors, then which one of the following statements can be false?

    (A) There are family cars on floor 1.
    (B) There are research models on floor 1.
    (C) There are new cars on floor 2.
    (D) There are research models on floor 2.
    (E) There are family cars on floor 3.

18. If all the new cars in the exhibition are research models, then which one of the following statements must be true?

    (A) All the family cars in the exhibition are new.
    (B) All the family cars in the exhibition are research models.
    (C) All the family cars in the exhibition are used.
    (D) All the new cars in the exhibition are family cars.
    (E) All the production models in the exhibition are family cars.

19. If all the production models in the exhibition are used, then which one of the following statements must be true?

    (A) There are family cars on floor 1.
    (B) There are new cars on floor 2.
    (C) There are research models on floor 2.
    (D) There are family cars on floor 3.
    (E) There are sports cars on floor 3.

A street cleaning crew works only Monday to Friday, and only during the day. It takes the crew an entire morning or an entire afternoon to clean a street. During one week the crew cleaned exactly eight streets—First, Second, Third, Fourth, Fifth, Sixth, Seventh, and Eighth streets. The following is known about the crew's schedule for the week:

The crew cleaned no street on Friday morning.
The crew cleaned no street on Wednesday afternoon.
It cleaned Fourth Street on Tuesday morning.
It cleaned Seventh Street on Thursday morning.
It cleaned Fourth Street before Sixth Street and after Eighth Street.
It cleaned Second, Fifth, and Eighth streets on afternoons.

12. If the crew cleaned Second Street earlier in the week than Seventh Street, then it must have cleaned which one of the following streets on Tuesday afternoon?

   (A) First Street
   (B) Second Street
   (C) Third Street
   (D) Fifth Street
   (E) Eighth Street

13. If the crew cleaned Sixth Street on a morning and cleaned Second Street before Seventh Street, then what is the maximum number of streets whose cleaning times cannot be determined?

   (A) 1
   (B) 2
   (C) 3
   (D) 4
   (E) 5

14. What is the maximum possible number of streets any one of which could be the one the crew cleaned on Friday afternoon?

   (A) 1
   (B) 2
   (C) 3
   (D) 4
   (E) 5

15. If the crew cleaned First Street earlier in the week than Third Street, then which one of the following statements must be false?

   (A) The crew cleaned First Street on Tuesday afternoon.
   (B) The crew cleaned Second Street on Thursday afternoon.
   (C) The crew cleaned Third Street on Wednesday morning.
   (D) The crew cleaned Fifth Street on Thursday afternoon.
   (E) The crew cleaned Sixth Street on Friday afternoon.

16. If the crew cleaned Fifth, Sixth, and Seventh streets in numerical order, then what is the maximum number of different schedules any one of which the crew could have had for the entire week?

   (A) 1
   (B) 2
   (C) 3
   (D) 4
   (E) 5

17. Suppose the crew had cleaned Fourth Street on Tuesday afternoon instead of on Tuesday morning, but all other conditions remained the same. Which one of the following statements could be false?

   (A) The crew cleaned First Street before Second Street.
   (B) The crew cleaned Second Street before Fifth Street.
   (C) The crew cleaned Third Street before Second Street.
   (D) The crew cleaned Sixth Street before Fifth Street.
   (E) The crew cleaned Seventh Street before Second Street.

A committee ranks five towns—Palmdale, Quietville, Riverdale, Seaside, Tidetown—from first (best) to fifth (worst) on each of three criteria: climate, location, friendliness.

For each of the three criteria, none of the five towns receives the same ranking as any other town does.

In climate, Tidetown is ranked third, and Seaside fourth.

In location, Quietville is ranked second, Riverdale third, Palmdale fourth.

In friendliness, Tidetown's ranking is better than Palmdale's, Quietville is ranked fourth, and Seaside fifth.

Riverdale receives a better ranking in climate than in friendliness.

Quietville's three rankings are all different from each other.

18. Which one of the following is a complete and accurate list of the rankings any one of which could be the ranking on climate given to Riverdale?

(A) first
(B) first, second
(C) first, fifth
(D) second, fifth
(E) first, second, fifth

19. Which one of the following is a town that CANNOT be ranked fifth on any one of the three criteria?

(A) Palmdale
(B) Quietville
(C) Riverdale
(D) Seaside
(E) Tidetown

20. Which one of the following could be true?

(A) Palmdale is ranked first in both climate and friendliness.
(B) Quietville is ranked second in both climate and location.
(C) Riverdale is ranked first in climate and third in both location and friendliness.
(D) Seaside is ranked fifth in friendliness and fourth in both climate and location.
(E) Tidetown is ranked third in both climate and friendliness.

21. If Quietville is ranked first in climate, then it must be true that

(A) Palmdale is ranked second in climate
(B) Palmdale is ranked third in friendliness
(C) Riverdale is ranked second in friendliness
(D) Riverdale is ranked third in friendliness
(E) Tidetown is ranked fifth in location

22. If Palmdale is ranked second in climate, then which one of the following can be true?

(A) Palmdale is ranked second in friendliness.
(B) Quietville is ranked first in climate.
(C) Riverdale is ranked first in friendliness.
(D) Riverdale is ranked fifth in climate.
(E) Tidetown is ranked third in friendliness.

23. If Tidetown is ranked first in location and Riverdale is ranked second in friendliness, then it is possible to deduce with certainty all three rankings for exactly how many of the towns?

(A) One
(B) Two
(C) Three
(D) Four
(E) Five

24. Which one of the following statements CANNOT be true?

(A) Palmdale is ranked first in climate.
(B) Quietville is ranked fifth in climate.
(C) Riverdale is ranked third in friendliness.
(D) Seaside is ranked first in location.
(E) Tidetown is ranked second in friendliness.

Doctor Yamata works only on Mondays, Tuesdays, Wednesdays, Fridays, and Saturdays. She performs four different activities—lecturing, operating, treating patients, and conducting research. Each working day she performs exactly one activity in the morning and exactly one activity in the afternoon. During each week her work schedule must satisfy the following restrictions:

> She performs operations on exactly three mornings.
> If she operates on Monday, she does not operate on Tuesday.
> She lectures in the afternoon on exactly two consecutive calendar days.
> She treats patients on exactly one morning and exactly three afternoons.
> She conducts research on exactly one morning.
> On Saturday she neither lectures nor performs operations.

8. Which one of the following must be a day on which Doctor Yamata lectures?

   (A) Monday
   (B) Tuesday
   (C) Wednesday
   (D) Friday
   (E) Saturday

9. On Wednesday Doctor Yamata could be scheduled to

   (A) conduct research in the morning and operate in the afternoon
   (B) lecture in the morning and treat patients in the afternoon
   (C) operate in the morning and lecture in the afternoon
   (D) operate in the morning and conduct research in the afternoon
   (E) treat patients in the morning and treat patients in the afternoon

10. Which one of the following statements must be true?

    (A) There is one day on which the doctor treats patients both in the morning and in the afternoon.
    (B) The doctor conducts research on one of the days on which she lectures.
    (C) The doctor conducts research on one of the days on which she treats patients.
    (D) The doctor lectures on one of the days on which she treats patients.
    (E) The doctor lectures on one of the days on which she operates.

11. If Doctor Yamata operates on Tuesday, then her schedule for treating patients could be

    (A) Monday morning, Monday afternoon, Friday morning, Friday afternoon
    (B) Monday morning, Friday afternoon, Saturday morning, Saturday afternoon
    (C) Monday afternoon, Wednesday morning, Wednesday afternoon, Saturday afternoon
    (D) Wednesday morning, Wednesday afternoon, Friday afternoon, Saturday afternoon
    (E) Wednesday afternoon, Friday afternoon, Saturday morning, Saturday afternoon

12. Which one of the following is a pair of days on both of which Doctor Yamata must treat patients?

    (A) Monday and Tuesday
    (B) Monday and Saturday
    (C) Tuesday and Friday
    (D) Tuesday and Saturday
    (E) Friday and Saturday

Seven children are to be seated in seven chairs arranged in a row that runs from west to east. All seven children will face north. Four of the children are boys: Frank, Harry, Ivan, and Joel. Three are girls: Ruby, Sylvia, and Thelma. The children are assigned to chairs according to the following conditions:

Exactly one child sits in each chair.
No boy sits next to another boy.
Ivan sits next to and east of the fourth child in the row.
Sylvia sits east of Ivan.
Frank sits next to Ruby.

13. What is the maximum possible number of different pairs of chairs in which Frank and Ruby could sit?

(A)   one
(B)   two
(C)   three
(D)   four
(E)   five

14. Which one of the following statements must be false?

(A)   Both Harry and Joel sit east of Frank.
(B)   Both Harry and Ruby sit east of Frank.
(C)   Both Harry and Joel sit west of Frank.
(D)   Both Harry and Ruby sit west of Frank.
(E)   Both Joel and Ruby sit east of Frank.

15. If Thelma sits next to Ivan, and if Frank sits next to Thelma, which one of the following statements could be false?

(A)   Both Frank and Ivan sit east of Ruby.
(B)   Both Frank and Ruby sit west of Thelma.
(C)   Both Frank and Sylvia sit east of Ruby.
(D)   Both Frank and Thelma sit west of Sylvia.
(E)   Both Frank and Ruby sit west of Joel.

16. If Frank does not sit next to any child who sits next to Ivan, which one of the following statements could be true?

(A)   Harry sits west of Frank.
(B)   Joel sits west of Ivan.
(C)   Ruby sits west of Frank.
(D)   Thelma sits west of Frank.
(E)   Thelma sits west of Ruby.

17. If Frank sits east of Ruby, which one of the following pairs of children CANNOT sit next to each other?

(A)   Frank and Thelma
(B)   Harry and Ruby
(C)   Harry and Sylvia
(D)   Ivan and Ruby
(E)   Joel and Ruby

During each of the fall, winter, spring, and summer seasons of one year, Nikki and Otto each participate in exactly one of the following five sports: hockey, kayaking, mountaineering, running, and volleyball.

Each child participates in exactly four different sports during the year.

In the fall, each child participates in mountaineering, running, or volleyball.

In the winter, each child participates in hockey or volleyball.

In the spring, each child participates in kayaking, mountaineering, running, or volleyball.

In the summer, each child participates in kayaking, mountaineering, or volleyball.

Nikki and Otto do not participate in the same sport during the same season.

Otto's summer sport is volleyball.

19. Which one of the following statements must be true?

   (A)   Nikki's fall sport is running.
   (B)   Nikki's winter sport is volleyball.
   (C)   Nikki's spring sport is mountaineering.
   (D)   Otto's fall sport is mountaineering.
   (E)   Otto's spring sport is kayaking.

20. It CANNOT be true that both Nikki and Otto participate during the year in which one of the following sports?

   (A)   hockey
   (B)   kayaking
   (C)   mountaineering
   (D)   running
   (E)   volleyball

21. If Nikki's fall sport is running, then which one of the following statements must be true?

   (A)   Nikki's spring sport is kayaking.
   (B)   Nikki's summer sport is mountaineering.
   (C)   Otto's fall sport is mountaineering.
   (D)   Otto's spring sport is kayaking.
   (E)   Otto's spring sport is running.

22. Which one of the following statements could be true?

   (A)   Nikki's fall sport is neither mountaineering nor running.
   (B)   Nikki's spring sport is neither mountaineering nor running.
   (C)   Nikki's summer sport is neither kayaking nor mountaineering.
   (D)   Otto's fall sport is neither mountaineering nor running.
   (E)   Otto's spring sport is neither kayaking, nor mountaineering, nor running.

23. If Otto does not run during the year, then which one of the following statements must be false?

   (A)   Nikki's fall sport is running.
   (B)   Nikki's spring sport is running.
   (C)   Nikki's summer sport is kayaking.
   (D)   Otto's fall sport is mountaineering.
   (E)   Otto's spring sport is kayaking.

24. Which one of the following statements could be true?

   (A)   Nikki's fall sport is mountaineering and Otto's spring sport is running.
   (B)   Nikki's spring sport is running and her summer sport is mountaineering.
   (C)   Nikki's spring sport is mountaineering and Otto's fall sport is mountaineering.
   (D)   Nikki's spring sport is running and Otto's fall sport is mountaineering.
   (E)   Nikki's summer sport is mountaineering and Otto's spring sport is mountaineering.

On an undeveloped street, a developer will simultaneously build four houses on one side, numbered consecutively 1, 3, 5, and 7, and four houses on the opposite side, numbered consecutively 2, 4, 6, and 8. Houses 2, 4, 6, and 8 will face houses 1, 3, 5, and 7, respectively. Each house will be exactly one of three styles—ranch, split-level, or Tudor—according to the following conditions:

 Adjacent houses are of different styles.
 No split-level house faces another split-level house.
 Every ranch house has at least one Tudor house
  adjacent to it.
 House 3 is a ranch house.
 House 6 is a split-level house.

13. Any of the following could be a Tudor house EXCEPT house

(A)   1
(B)   2
(C)   4
(D)   7
(E)   8

14. If there is one ranch house directly opposite another ranch house, which one of the following could be true?

(A)   House 8 is a ranch house.
(B)   House 7 is a split-level house.
(C)   House 4 is a Tudor house.
(D)   House 2 is a split-level house.
(E)   House 1 is a ranch house.

15. If house 4 is a Tudor house, then it could be true that house

(A)   1 is a Tudor house
(B)   2 is a Tudor house
(C)   5 is a ranch house
(D)   7 is a Tudor house
(E)   8 is a ranch house

16. On the street, there could be exactly

(A)   one ranch house
(B)   one Tudor house
(C)   two Tudor houses
(D)   four ranch houses
(E)   five ranch houses

17. If no house faces a house of the same style, then it must be true that house

(A)   1 is a split-level house
(B)   1 is a Tudor house
(C)   2 is a ranch house
(D)   2 is a split-level house
(E)   4 is a Tudor house

18. If the condition requiring house 6 to be a split-level house is suspended but all other original conditions remain the same, then any of the following could be an accurate list of the styles of houses 2, 4, 6, and 8, respectively, EXCEPT:

(A)   ranch, split-level, ranch, Tudor
(B)   split-level, ranch, Tudor, split-level
(C)   split-level, Tudor, ranch, split-level
(D)   Tudor, ranch, Tudor, split-level
(E)   Tudor, split-level, ranch, Tudor

ADVANCED LINEAR

On Tuesday Vladimir and Wendy each eat exactly four separate meals: breakfast, lunch, dinner, and a snack. The following is all that is known about what they eat during that day:

At no meal does Vladimir eat the same kind of food as Wendy.

Neither of them eats the same kind of food more than once during the day.

For breakfast, each eats exactly one of the following: hot cakes, poached eggs, or omelet.

For lunch, each eats exactly one of the following: fish, hot cakes, macaroni, or omelet.

For dinner, each eats exactly one of the following: fish, hot cakes, macaroni, or omelet.

For a snack, each eats exactly one of the following: fish or omelet.

Wendy eats an omelet for lunch.

13. Which one of the following statements must be true?

(A)   Vladimir eats fish for lunch.
(B)   Vladimir eats fish for dinner.
(C)   Vladimir eats fish for his snack.
(D)   Wendy eats fish for dinner.
(E)   Wendy eats fish for her snack.

14. Vladimir must eat which one of the following foods?

(A)   fish
(B)   hot cakes
(C)   macaroni
(D)   omelet
(E)   poached eggs

15. If both Vladimir and Wendy eat macaroni on Tuesday, then which one of the following statements could be true?

(A)   Vladimir eats fish for lunch.
(B)   Vladimir eats hot cakes for lunch.
(C)   Vladimir eats macaroni for dinner.
(D)   Wendy eats hot cakes for breakfast.
(E)   Wendy eats hot cakes for dinner.

16. If Wendy does not eat macaroni on Tuesday, then which one of the following statements could be true?

(A)   Vladimir eats poached eggs for breakfast.
(B)   Vladimir eats fish for lunch.
(C)   Vladimir eats hot cakes for lunch.
(D)   Wendy eats hot cakes for breakfast.
(E)   Wendy eats fish for dinner.

17. If Wendy eats poached eggs for breakfast, then which one of the following statements cannot be true?

(A)   Vladimir eats fish for lunch.
(B)   Vladimir eats hot cakes for lunch.
(C)   Vladimir eats macaroni for dinner.
(D)   Wendy eats hot cakes for dinner.
(E)   Wendy eats macaroni for dinner.

Each of seven travelers—Norris, Oribe, Paulsen, Rosen, Semonelli, Tan, and Underwood—will be assigned to exactly one of nine airplane seats. The seats are numbered from 1 through 9 and arranged in rows as follows:

Front row: 1   2   3
Middle row: 4   5   6
Last row: 7   8   9

Only seats in the same row as each other are immediately beside each other. Seat assignments must meet the following conditions:

Oribe's seat is in the last row.
Paulsen's seat is immediately beside Rosen's seat and also immediately beside an unassigned seat.
Rosen's seat is in the row immediately behind the row in which Norris' seat is located.
Neither Semonelli nor Underwood is seated immediately beside Norris.

1. Which one of the following is a pair of travelers who could be assigned to seats 2 and 8, respectively?

    (A)   Norris, Semonelli
    (B)   Oribe, Underwood
    (C)   Paulsen, Oribe
    (D)   Rosen, Semonelli
    (E)   Underwood, Tan

2. If Semonelli and Underwood are not assigned to seats in the same row as each other, which one of the following must be false?

    (A)   Norris is assigned to seat 2.
    (B)   Paulsen is assigned to seat 5.
    (C)   Rosen is assigned to seat 4.
    (D)   Tan is assigned to seat 2.
    (E)   Underwood is assigned to seat 1.

3. If Semonelli is assigned to a seat in the same row as Underwood, which one of the following travelers could be assigned to a seat immediately beside one of the unassigned seats?

    (A)   Oribe
    (B)   Rosen
    (C)   Semonelli
    (D)   Tan
    (E)   Underwood

4. If the seat to which Tan is assigned is immediately beside a seat assigned to another traveler and also immediately beside one of the unassigned seats, which one of the following must be true?

    (A)   Tan is assigned to a seat in the front row.
    (B)   Tan is assigned to a seat in the last row.
    (C)   Oribe is assigned to a seat immediately beside Semonelli.
    (D)   Oribe is assigned to a seat immediately beside Tan.
    (E)   Semonelli is assigned to a seat immediately beside Underwood.

5. If Oribe is assigned to a seat immediately beside one of the unassigned seats, which one of the following must be true?

    (A)   Oribe is assigned to seat 8.
    (B)   Tan is assigned to seat 2.
    (C)   Underwood is assigned to seat 1.
    (D)   Seat 4 is unassigned.
    (E)   Seat 9 is unassigned.

ADVANCED LINEAR

Chapter Four:
Grouping Games

Chapter Four: Grouping Games

Three couples—John and Kate, Lewis and Marie, and Nat and Olive—have dinner in a restaurant together. Kate, Marie, and Olive are women; the other three are men. Each person orders one and only one of the following kinds of entrees: pork chops, roast beef, swordfish, tilefish, veal cutlet. The six people order in a manner consistent with the following conditions:

> The two people in each couple do not order the same kind of entree as each other.
> None of the men orders the same kind of entree as any of the other men.
> Marie orders swordfish.
> Neither John nor Nat orders a fish entree.
> Olive orders roast beef.

1. Which one of the following is a complete and accurate list of the entrees any one of which Lewis could order?

    (A) pork chops, roast beef
    (B) pork chops, veal cutlet
    (C) pork chops, swordfish, veal cutlet
    (D) pork chops, roast beef, tilefish, veal cutlet
    (E) pork chops, roast beef, swordfish, tilefish, veal cutlet

2. Which one of the following statements could be true?

    (A) John orders the same kind of entree as Marie does.
    (B) Kate orders the same kind of entree as Nat does.
    (C) Lewis orders the same kind of entree as Nat does.
    (D) Marie orders the same kind of entree as Olive does.
    (E) Nat orders the same kind of entree as Olive does.

3. Which one of the following statements must be true?

    (A) One of the men orders pork chops or veal cutlet.
    (B) One of the men orders swordfish or veal cutlet.
    (C) Two of the women order tilefish.
    (D) None of the men orders a fish entree.
    (E) Exactly one of the women orders a fish entree.

4. If John orders veal cutlet, then which one of the following statements must be true?

    (A) Kate orders roast beef.
    (B) Kate orders swordfish.
    (C) Lewis orders tilefish.
    (D) Lewis orders veal cutlet.
    (E) Nat orders pork chops.

5. If none of the six people orders pork chops, then which one of the following statements must be true?

    (A) John orders veal cutlet.
    (B) Kate orders tilefish.
    (C) Lewis orders tilefish.
    (D) One of the men orders swordfish.
    (E) One of the women orders tilefish.

6. If Lewis orders pork chops, then which one of the following is a complete and accurate list of the entrees any one of which John could order?

    (A) roast beef
    (B) veal cutlet
    (C) roast beef, veal cutlet
    (D) roast beef, swordfish
    (E) pork chops, roast beef, swordfish

7. Suppose that the people in each couple both order the same kind of entree as each other rather than order different kinds of entrees. If all other conditions remain the same, and no two women order the same kind of entree, then which one of the following statements could be true?

    (A) John orders roast beef.
    (B) John orders swordfish.
    (C) Kate orders roast beef.
    (D) Two of the people order pork chops.
    (E) Two of the people order tilefish.

Planes 1, 2, 3, and 4—and no others—are available to fly in an air show.

Pilots Anna, Bob, and Cindy are all aboard planes that are flying in the show and they are the only qualified pilots in the show.

Copilots Dave, Ed, and Fran are all aboard planes that are flying in the show and they are the only qualified copilots in the show.

No plane flies in the show without a qualified pilot aboard.

No one but qualified pilots and qualified copilots flies in the show.

Anna will only fly in either plane 1 or plane 4.

Dave will only fly in either plane 2 or plane 3.

20. If Anna flies in Plane 4 and Dave flies in plane 2, which one of the following must be true?

   (A)   Cindy flies in either plane 1 or plane 3.
   (B)   If Cindy flies in plane 3, Bob flies in plane 2.
   (C)   Bob and one other person fly in plane 1.
   (D)   If Bob is aboard plane 4, Cindy flies in plane 3.
   (E)   If Cindy is in plane 2, Bob flies in plane 3.

21. If Bob and Anna fly on the same plane, which one of the following must be true?

   (A)   Cindy flies with Dave and Ed.
   (B)   Cindy flies with Ed.
   (C)   Dave flies with Cindy.
   (D)   Dave flies with Cindy, Ed, and Fran.
   (E)   Fran flies with Ed.

22. If Cindy and Fran are the only people in one of the planes, which one of the following must be true?

   (A)   Bob flies with Anna.
   (B)   Dave flies with Ed.
   (C)   Dave and Ed fly with Bob.
   (D)   Dave flies with Bob.
   (E)   Ed flies with Anna.

23. If plane 1 is used, its crew could consist of

   (A)   Anna, Bob, Cindy, Fran
   (B)   Anna, Bob, Ed, Fran
   (C)   Bob, Cindy, Ed, Fran
   (D)   Bob, Cindy, Dave, Ed
   (E)   Bob, Dave, Ed, Fran

24. If as many of the pilots and copilots as possible fly in plane 4, that group will consist of

   (A)   exactly two people
   (B)   exactly three people
   (C)   exactly four people
   (D)   exactly five people
   (E)   three pilots and two copilots

GROUPING

Each of five illnesses—J, K, L, M, and N—is characterized by at least one of the following three symptoms: fever, headache, and sneezing. None of the illnesses has any symptom that is not one of these three.

  Illness J is characterized by headache and sneezing.
  Illnesses J and K have no symptoms in common.
  Illnesses J and L have at least one symptom in common.
  Illness L has a greater number of symptoms than illness K.
  Illnesses L and N have no symptoms in common.
  Illness M has more symptoms than illness J.

7. Which one of the following statements must be false?

    (A)   Illness J has exactly two symptoms.
    (B)   Illness K has exactly one symptom.
    (C)   Illness L has exactly two symptoms.
    (D)   Illness M has exactly three symptoms.
    (E)   Illness N has exactly two symptoms.

8. In which one of the following pairs could the first member of the pair be characterized by exactly the same number and types of symptoms as the second member of the pair?

    (A)   J and N
    (B)   K and L
    (C)   K and N
    (D)   L and M
    (E)   M and N

9. If illness L is characterized by a combination of symptoms different from any of the other illnesses, then which one of the following statements must be true?

    (A)   Fever is a symptom of illness L.
    (B)   Sneezing is a symptom of illness L.
    (C)   Headache is a symptom of illness L.
    (D)   Illnesses K and N are characterized by exactly the same symptoms.
    (E)   Illnesses M and N are characterized by exactly the same symptoms.

10. The illnesses in which one of the following pairs must have exactly one symptom in common?

    (A)   J and L
    (B)   J and M
    (C)   J and N
    (D)   K and L
    (E)   M and N

11. If Walter has exactly two of the three symptoms, then he cannot have all of the symptoms of

    (A)   both illness J and illness L
    (B)   both illness J and illness N
    (C)   both illness K and illness L
    (D)   both illness K and illness N
    (E)   both illness L and illness N

A store sells shirts only in small, medium, and large sizes, and only in red, yellow, and blue colors. Casey buys exactly three shirts from the store.

A shirt type consists of both a size and a color.
Casey does not buy two shirts of the same type.
Casey does not buy both a small shirt and a large shirt.
No small red shirts are available.
No large blue shirts are available.

7. Which one of the following must be false?

   (A) Two of the shirts that Casey buys are small and two are red.
   (B) Two of the shirts that Casey buys are medium and two are red.
   (C) Two of the shirts that Casey buys are large and two are red.
   (D) Two of the shirts that Casey buys are small, one is yellow, and one is blue.
   (E) Two of the shirts that Casey buys are medium, one is yellow, and one is blue.

8. If Casey buys a small blue shirt, which one of the following must be false?

   (A) Casey buys two blue shirts.
   (B) Casey buys two red shirts.
   (C) Casey buys two yellow shirts.
   (D) Casey buys two small shirts.
   (E) Casey buys two medium shirts.

9. If Casey does not buy a medium yellow shirt, which one of the following must be true?

   (A) Casey buys either a medium red shirt or a small blue shirt.
   (B) Casey buys either a medium red shirt or a medium blue shirt.
   (C) Casey buys either a large red shirt or a small blue shirt.
   (D) Casey buys either a large red shirt or a medium red shirt.
   (E) Casey buys either a large yellow shirt or a small yellow shirt.

10. If Casey buys exactly one medium shirt and does not buy two shirts of the same color, then she cannot buy which one of the following?

   (A) a medium red shirt
   (B) a medium yellow shirt
   (C) a medium blue shirt
   (D) a large red shirt
   (E) a large yellow shirt

11. If neither large red shirts nor small blue shirts are available, which one of the following must Casey buy?

   (A) a red shirt
   (B) a medium yellow shirt
   (C) either a large shirt or a small shirt
   (D) either a medium red shirt or a medium blue shirt
   (E) either a large yellow shirt or a medium blue shirt

A hobbyist is stocking her aquarium with exactly three fish of different types and with exactly two species of plants. The only fish under consideration are a G, an H, a J, a K, and an L, and the only kinds of plants under consideration are of the species W, X, Y, and Z. She will observe the following conditions:

If she selects the G, she can select neither the H nor a Y.

She cannot select the H unless she selects the K.

She cannot select the J unless she selects a W.

If she selects the K, she must select an X.

12. Which one of the following is an acceptable selection of fish and plants for the aquarium?

	Fish	Plants
(A)	G, H, K	W, Y
(B)	G, J, K	W, X
(C)	G, J, L	X, Z
(D)	H, J, L	W, Z
(E)	H, K, L	Y, Z

13. If the hobbyist selects the H, which one of the following must also be true?

(A) She selects at least one W.
(B) She selects at least one X.
(C) She selects the J, but no Y's.
(D) She selects the K, but no X's.
(E) She selects at least one X, but no Y's.

14. If the hobbyist selects both X's and Z's, which one of the following could be the group of fish she selects?

(A) G, H, K
(B) G, J, K
(C) G, K, L
(D) H, J, L
(E) J, K, L

15. The hobbyist could select any of the following groups of fish for the aquarium EXCEPT

(A) G, K, L
(B) H, J, K
(C) H, J, L
(D) H, K, L
(E) J, K, L

16. If the hobbyist selects a Y, which one of the following must be the group of fish she selects?

(A) G, H, K
(B) H, J, K
(C) H, J, L
(D) H, K, L
(E) J, K, L

17. The hobbyist could select any of the following plant combinations EXCEPT

(A) W and X
(B) W and Y
(C) W and Z
(D) X and Y
(E) X and Z

GROUPING

The organisms W, X, Y, and Z respond to the antibiotics ferromycin, ganocyclene, and heptocillin in a manner consistent with the following:

Each of the organisms responds to at least one of the antibiotics.

No organism responds to all three antibiotics.

At least two but not all four of the organisms respond to ferromycin.

If W responds to any antibiotic, then X responds to that antibiotic.

If an organism responds to ferromycin, then it responds to ganocyclene.

Y responds to ferromycin.

18. Each of the following can be true EXCEPT:

   (A) W responds to heptocillin.
   (B) X responds to ganocyclene.
   (C) X responds to heptocillin.
   (D) Y responds to heptocillin.
   (E) Z responds to ganocyclene.

19. Which one of the following could be true?

   (A) W, X, and Z all respond to ferromycin.
   (B) W, X, and Z all respond to ganocyclene.
   (C) W and exactly one other organism respond to ganocyclene.
   (D) W responds to more of the antibiotics than X does.
   (E) More of the organisms respond to ferromycin than to ganocyclene.

20. Which one of the following could be true?

   (A) Exactly one of the organisms responds to ferromycin.
   (B) All four of the organisms respond to heptocillin.
   (C) At least one of the organisms responds both to ferromycin and to heptocillin.
   (D) At least one of the organisms responds neither to ganocyclene nor to heptocillin.
   (E) At least one of the organisms responds to ganocyclene but does not respond to ferromycin.

21. If X does not respond to ferromycin, then which one of the following must be true?

   (A) W responds to ganocyclene.
   (B) X responds to ganocyclene.
   (C) X responds to heptocillin.
   (D) Z responds to ferromycin.
   (E) Z responds to heptocillin.

22. If any of the organisms responds to two of the antibiotics, then which one of the following is true about such an organism?

   (A) It must respond to ferromycin.
   (B) It must respond to ganocyclene.
   (C) It must respond to heptocillin.
   (D) It cannot respond to ferromycin.
   (E) It cannot respond to ganocyclene.

23. If none of the organisms responds to heptocillin, then which one of the following must be true?

   (A) W responds to ferromycin.
   (B) X responds to ferromycin.
   (C) Z responds to ferromycin.
   (D) Exactly three of the organisms respond to ganocyclene.
   (E) Exactly four of the organisms respond to ganocyclene.

24. If three of the organisms respond to exactly the same set of antibiotics as each other, and if Z does not respond to ferromycin, then each of the following must be true EXCEPT:

   (A) W responds to ferromycin.
   (B) X responds to ganocyclene.
   (C) Z responds to ganocyclene.
   (D) W responds to exactly the same set of antibiotics as Y.
   (E) X responds to exactly the same set of antibiotics as Y.

From a group of seven people—J, K, L, M, N, P, and Q—exactly four will be selected to attend a diplomat's retirement dinner. Selection must conform to the following conditions:

Either J or K must be selected, but J and K cannot both be selected.

Either N or P must be selected, but N and P cannot both be selected.

N cannot be selected unless L is selected.

Q cannot be selected unless K is selected.

8. Which one of the following could be the four people selected to attend the retirement dinner?

(A) J, K, M, P
(B) J, L, N, Q
(C) J, M, N, Q
(D) K, M, P, Q
(E) L, M, N, P

9. Among the people selected to attend the retirement dinner there must be

(A) K or Q or both
(B) L or M or both
(C) N or M or both
(D) N or Q or both
(E) P or Q or both

10. Which one of the following is a pair of people who CANNOT both be selected to attend the retirement dinner?

(A) J and N
(B) J and Q
(C) K and L
(D) K and N
(E) N and Q

11. If M is not selected to attend the retirement dinner, the four people selected to attend must include which one of the following pairs of people?

(A) J and Q
(B) K and L
(C) K and P
(D) L and P
(E) N and Q

12. If P is not selected to attend the retirement dinner, then exactly how many different groups of four are there each of which would be an acceptable selection?

(A) one
(B) two
(C) three
(D) four
(E) five

13. There is only one acceptable group of four that can be selected to attend the retirement dinner if which one of the following pairs of people is selected?

(A) J and L
(B) K and M
(C) L and N
(D) L and Q
(E) M and Q

GROUPING

Game #8: June 1994 Questions 1-6

Eight camp counselors—Fran, George, Henry, Joan, Kathy, Lewis, Nathan, and Olga—must each be assigned to supervise exactly one of three activities—swimming, tennis, and volleyball. The assignment of counselors must conform to the following conditions:

Each activity is supervised by at least two, but not more than three, of the eight counselors.

Henry supervises swimming.

Neither Kathy nor Olga supervises tennis.

Neither Kathy nor Nathan supervises the same activity as Joan.

If George supervises swimming, both Nathan and Olga supervise volleyball.

1. Which one of the following is an acceptable assignment of the counselors to the activities?

   (A) Swimming: Fran, George, Henry; Tennis: Joan, Lewis; Volleyball: Kathy, Nathan, Olga
   (B) Swimming: George, Henry, Olga; Tennis: Fran, Joan, Lewis; Volleyball: Kathy, Nathan
   (C) Swimming: Henry; Tennis: Fran, George, Joan, Lewis; Volleyball: Kathy, Nathan, Olga
   (D) Swimming: Henry, Joan, Kathy; Tennis: George, Nathan; Volleyball: Fran, Lewis, Olga
   (E) Swimming: Henry, Nathan; Tennis: Fran, Kathy, Lewis; Volleyball: George, Joan, Olga

2. Which one of the following is a pair of counselors who could be two of three counselors assigned to supervise swimming?

   (A) George and Nathan
   (B) George and Olga
   (C) Joan and Kathy
   (D) Joan and Nathan
   (E) Joan and Olga

3. Which one of the following is a pair of counselors who could together be assigned to supervise tennis?

   (A) Fran and Kathy
   (B) George and Nathan
   (C) Henry and Lewis
   (D) Joan and Nathan
   (E) Joan and Olga

4. If George and Kathy are two of three counselors assigned to supervise swimming, which one of the following could be true of the assignment?

   (A) Fran supervises swimming.
   (B) Henry supervises tennis.
   (C) Joan supervises volleyball.
   (D) Lewis supervises volleyball.
   (E) Nathan supervises tennis.

5. If Fran and Lewis are two of three counselors assigned to supervise swimming, which one of the following must be true of the assignment?

   (A) George supervises volleyball.
   (B) Henry supervises volleyball.
   (C) Joan supervises tennis.
   (D) Kathy supervises swimming.
   (E) Nathan supervises tennis.

6. If Joan is assigned to supervise the same activity as Olga, which one of the following CANNOT be true of the assignment?

   (A) Fran supervises swimming.
   (B) George supervises swimming.
   (C) Kathy supervises volleyball.
   (D) Lewis supervises volleyball.
   (E) Nathan supervises tennis.

A housing committee will consist of exactly five representatives, one of whom will be its chairperson. The representatives will be selected from among a group of five tenants—F, G, J, K, and M—and a group of four homeowners—P, Q, R, and S. The following conditions must be met:

> The committee must include at least two representatives from each group.
> The chairperson must be a representative belonging to the group from which exactly two representatives are selected.
> If F is selected, Q must be selected.
> If G is selected, K must be selected.
> If either J or M is selected, the other must also be selected.
> M and P cannot both be selected.

12. Which one of the following is an acceptable selection of representatives for the committee?

    (A) F, G, Q, R, S
    (B) F, J, K, P, Q
    (C) F, P, Q, R, S
    (D) J, K, M, Q, S
    (E) J, M, P, Q, S

13. Which one of the following lists three representatives who could be selected together for the committee?

    (A) F, G, J
    (B) F, G, M
    (C) F, J, M
    (D) G, J, K
    (E) G, J, M

14. If M is the chairperson of the committee, which one of the following is among the people who must also be on the committee?

    (A) F
    (B) G
    (C) K
    (D) P
    (E) R

15. If F is the chairperson of the committee, which one of the following is among the people who must also be on the committee?

    (A) G
    (B) K
    (C) P
    (D) R
    (E) S

16. If F is selected, any one of the following people could be the chairperson of the committee EXCEPT:

    (A) G
    (B) K
    (C) P
    (D) Q
    (E) S

17. If neither F nor K is selected for the committee, which one of the following can be true?

    (A) G is selected.
    (B) P is selected.
    (C) J is the chairperson.
    (D) Q is the chairperson.
    (E) S is the chairperson.

18. If the chairperson of the committee is to be a homeowner, which one of the following must be true?

    (A) If G is selected, Q is also selected.
    (B) If G is selected, R is also selected.
    (C) If J is selected, F is also selected.
    (D) If J is selected, Q is also selected.
    (E) If J is selected, R is also selected.

19. The committee must include at least one representative from which one of the following pairs?

    (A) F, P
    (B) G, J
    (C) K, Q
    (D) M, P
    (E) R, S

Five children—F, G, H, J, and K—and four adults—Q, R, S, and T—are planning a canoeing trip. The canoeists will be divided into three groups—groups 1, 2, and 3—of three canoeists each, according to the following conditions:

There must be at least one adult in each group.
F must be in the same group as J.
G cannot be in the same group as T.
H cannot be in the same group as R.
Neither H nor T can be in group 2.

7. If F is in group 1, which one of the following could be true?

(A) G and K are in group 3.
(B) G and R are in group 3.
(C) J and S are in group 2.
(D) K and R are in group 1.
(E) Q and S are in group 2.

8. If F and S are in group 3, which one of the following must be true?

(A) G is in group 2.
(B) H is in group 3.
(C) K is in group 1.
(D) Q is in group 2.
(E) R is in group 1.

9. If G and K are in group 3, which one of the following must be true?

(A) H is in group 3.
(B) J is in group 1.
(C) R is in group 2.
(D) S is in group 3.
(E) T is in group 1.

10. If Q is in group 1 and S is in group 3, which one of the following CANNOT be true?

(A) G is in group 2.
(B) T is in group 1.
(C) There is exactly one child in group 1.
(D) There is exactly one child in group 2.
(E) There is exactly one child in group 3.

11. If G is the only child in group 1, which one of the following must be true?

(A) F is in group 3.
(B) K is in group 3.
(C) Q is in group 2.
(D) R is in group 1.
(E) S is in group 2.

Lara, Mendel, and Nastassia each buy at least one kind of food from a street vendor who sells only fruit cups, hot dogs, pretzels, and shish kebabs. They make their selections in accordance with the following restrictions:

  None of the three buys more than one portion of each kind of food.

  If any of the three buys a hot dog, that person does not also buy a shish kebab.

  At least one of the three buys a hot dog, and at least one buys a pretzel.

  Mendel buys a shish kebab.

  Nastassia buys a fruit cup.

  Neither Lara nor Nastassia buys a pretzel.

  Mendel does not buy any kind of food that Nastassia buys.

12. Which one of the following statements must be true?

  (A)   Lara buys a hot dog.
  (B)   Lara buys a shish kebab.
  (C)   Mendel buys a hot dog.
  (D)   Mendel buys a pretzel.
  (E)   Nastassia buys a hot dog.

13. If the vendor charges $1 for each portion of food, what is the minimum amount the three people could spend?

  (A) $3
  (B) $4
  (C) $5
  (D) $6
  (E) $7

14. If the vendor charges $1 for each portion of food, what is the greatest amount the three people could spend?

  (A) $5
  (B) $6
  (C) $7
  (D) $8
  (E) $9

15. If Lara and Mendel buy exactly two kinds of food each, which one of the following statements must be true?

  (A)   Lara buys a fruit cup.
  (B)   Lara buys a hot dog.
  (C)   Mendel buys a fruit cup.
  (D)   There is exactly one kind of food that Lara and Mendel both buy.
  (E)   There is exactly one kind of food that Lara and Nastassia both buy.

16. If Lara buys a shish kebab, which one of the following statements must be true?

  (A)   Lara buys a fruit cup.
  (B)   Mendel buys a fruit cup.
  (C)   Nastassia buys a hot dog.
  (D)   Nastassia buys exactly one kind of food.
  (E)   Exactly one person buys a fruit cup.

17. Assume that the condition is removed that prevents a customer who buys a hot dog from buying a shish kebab but all other conditions remain the same. If the vendor charges $1 for each portion of food, what is the maximum amount the three people could spend?

  (A) $5
  (B) $6
  (C) $7
  (D) $8
  (E) $9

Exactly eight consumers—F, G, H, J, K, L, M, and N—will be interviewed by market researchers. The eight will be divided into exactly two 4-person groups—group 1 and group 2—before interviews begin. Each person is assigned to exactly one of the two groups according to the following conditions:

F must be in the same group as J.
G must be in a different group from M.
If H is in group 1, then L must be in group 1.
If N is in group 2, then G must be in group 1.

1. Group 1 could consist of

(A) F, G, H, and J
(B) F, H, L, and M
(C) F, J, K, and L
(D) G, H, L, and N
(E) G, K, M, and N

2. If K is in the same group as N, which one of the following must be true?

(A) G is in group 1.
(B) H is in group 2.
(C) J is in group 1.
(D) K is in group 2.
(E) M is in group 1.

3. If F is in the same group as H, which one of the following must be true?

(A) G is in group 2.
(B) J is in group 1.
(C) K is in group 1.
(D) L is in group 2.
(E) M is in group 2.

4. If L and M are in group 2, then a person who could be assigned either to group 1 or, alternatively, to group 2 is

(A) F
(B) G
(C) H
(D) J
(E) K

5. Each of the following is a pair of people who could be in group 1 together EXCEPT

(A) F and G
(B) F and H
(C) F and L
(D) H and G
(E) H and N

6. If L is in group 2, then each of the following is a pair of people who could be in group 1 together EXCEPT

(A) F and M
(B) G and N
(C) J and N
(D) K and M
(E) M and N

Game #13: February 1995 Questions 1-6

A newly formed company has five employees—F, G, H, K, and L. Each employee holds exactly one of the following positions: president, manager, or technician. Only the president is not supervised. Other employees are each supervised by exactly one employee, who is either the president or a manager. Each supervised employee holds a different position than his or her supervisor. The following conditions apply:

There is exactly one president.
At least one of the employees whom the president supervises is a manager.
Each manager supervises at least one employee.
F does not supervise any employee.
G supervises exactly two employees.

1. Which one of the following is an acceptable assignment of employees to the positions?

	President	Manager	Technician
(A)	G	H, K, L	F
(B)	G	H	F, K, L
(C)	H	F, G	K, L
(D)	H, K	G	F, L
(E)	K	F, G, H, L	-

2. Which one of the following must be true?

(A) There are at most three technicians.
(B) There is exactly one technician.
(C) There are at least two managers.
(D) There are exactly two managers.
(E) There are exactly two employees who supervise no one.

3. Which one of the following is a pair of employees who could serve as managers together?

(A) F, H
(B) F, L
(C) G, K
(D) G, L
(E) K, L

4. Which one of the following could be true?

(A) There is exactly one technician.
(B) There are exactly two managers.
(C) There are exactly two employees who are not supervised.
(D) There are more managers than technicians.
(E) The president supervises all of the other employees.

5. If F is supervised by the president, which one of the following must be true?

(A) G is the president.
(B) H is the president.
(C) L is a technician.
(D) There is exactly one manager.
(E) There are exactly two technicians.

6. If K supervises exactly two employees, which one of the following must be true?

(A) F is supervised by K.
(B) G is a manager.
(C) L is supervised.
(D) There are exactly two managers.
(E) There are exactly two technicians.

A breeder has ten birds:

Kind	Male	Female
Goldfinches	H	J, K
Lovebirds	M	N
Parakeets	Q, R, S	T, W

The breeder exhibits pairs of birds consisting of one male and one female of the same kind. At most two pairs can be exhibited at a time; the remaining birds must be distributed between two cages. The breeder is constrained by the following conditions:

Neither cage can contain more than four birds.

Any two birds that are both of the same sex and of the same kind as each other cannot be caged together.

Whenever either J or W is exhibited, S cannot be exhibited.

13. Which one of the following is a possible assignment of the birds?

	First Cage	Second Cage	Exhibition
(A)	H, M, N	J, K, S	Q, R, T, W
(B)	K, M, Q	N, R, W	H, J, S, T
(C)	K, Q, S	R, T, W	H, J, M, N
(D)	H, J, M, R	K, N, S, W	Q, T
(E)	H, J, M, R, W	K, N, S	Q, T, W

14. Which one of the following lists two pairs of birds that the breeder can exhibit at the same time?

(A) H and J; M and N
(B) H and J; S and T
(C) H and K; M and N
(D) H and K; R and W
(E) M and N; S and W

15. If Q and R are among the birds that are assigned to the cages, then it must be true that

(A) H is exhibited
(B) K is exhibited
(C) N is exhibited
(D) J is assigned to one of the cages
(E) T is assigned to one of the cages

16. If Q and T are among the birds assigned to the cages, which one of the following is a pair of birds that must be exhibited?

(A) H and J
(B) H and K
(C) M and N
(D) R and W
(E) S and W

17. Which one of the following CANNOT be true?

(A) One pair of parakeets are the only birds exhibited together.
(B) One pair of goldfinches and one pair of lovebirds are exhibited together.
(C) One pair of goldfinches and one pair of parakeets are exhibited together.
(D) One pair of lovebirds and one pair of parakeets are exhibited together.
(E) Two pairs of parakeets are exhibited together.

18. If S is one of the birds exhibited, it must be true that

(A) H is exhibited
(B) M is exhibited
(C) K is assigned to a cage
(D) N is assigned to a cage
(E) R is assigned to a cage

GROUPING

Game #15: June 1995 Questions 20-24

Five experienced plumbers—Frank, Gene, Jill, Kathy, and Mark—and four inexperienced plumbers—Roberta, Sally, Tim, and Vernon—must decide which of them will be assigned to four work teams of exactly two plumbers each. Assignments must meet the following restrictions:

Each plumber is assigned to at most one team.
At least one plumber on each team must be experienced.
Neither Mark nor Roberta nor Vernon can be assigned to a team with Frank.
If Tim is assigned to a team, either Gene or Kathy must be assigned to that team.
Jill cannot be assigned to a team with Roberta.

20. Which one of the following is an inexperienced plumber who can be assigned to a team with Frank?

(A) Kathy
(B) Roberta
(C) Sally
(D) Tim
(E) Vernon

21. Which one of the following is a pair of plumbers who can be assigned together to a team?

(A) Frank and Roberta
(B) Frank and Vernon
(C) Jill and Mark
(D) Roberta and Tim
(E) Sally and Vernon

22. If Tim is assigned to a team, and if Sally is assigned to a team with a plumber who could have been assigned to a team with Tim, then the only plumber with whom Frank could be assigned to a team is

(A) Gene
(B) Jill
(C) Mark
(D) Roberta
(E) Vernon

23. If Gene is not assigned to a team, then Jill must be assigned to a team with

(A) Vernon
(B) Tim
(C) Mark
(D) Kathy
(E) Frank

24. If all of the inexperienced plumbers are assigned to teams, and neither Roberta nor Tim nor Vernon is assigned to a team with Gene, then Sally must be assigned to a team with either

(A) Frank or else Gene
(B) Frank or else Mark
(C) Gene or else Mark
(D) Jill or else Kathy
(E) Jill or else Mark

Eight new students—R, S, T, V, W, X, Y, Z—are being divided among exactly three classes—class 1, class 2, and class 3. Classes 1 and 2 will gain three new students each; class 3 will gain two new students. The following restrictions apply:

R must be added to class 1.

S must be added to class 3.

Neither S nor W can be added to the same class as Y.

V cannot be added to the same class as Z.

If T is added to class 1, Z must also be added to class 1.

1. Which one of the following is an acceptable assignment of students to the three classes?

	1	2	3
(A)	R, T, Y	V, W, X	S, Z
(B)	R, T, Z	S, V, Y	W, X
(C)	R, W, X	V, Y, Z	S, T
(D)	R, X, Z	T, V, Y	S, W
(E)	R, X, Z	V, W, Y	S, T

2. Which one of the following is a complete and accurate list of classes any one of which could be the class to which V is added?

(A)   class 1
(B)   class 3
(C)   class 1, class 3
(D)   class 2, class 3
(E)   class 1, class 2, class 3

3. If X is added to class 1, which one of the following is a student who must be added to class 2?

(A)   T
(B)   V
(C)   W
(D)   Y
(E)   Z

4. If X is added to class 3, each of the following is a pair of students who can be added to class 1 EXCEPT

(A)   Y and Z
(B)   W and Z
(C)   V and Y
(D)   V and W
(E)   T and Z

5. If T is added to class 3, which one of the following is a student who must be added to class 2?

(A)   V
(B)   W
(C)   X
(D)   Y
(E)   Z

6. Which one of the following must be true?

(A)   If T and X are added to class 2, V is added to class 3.
(B)   If V and W are added to class 1, T is added to class 3.
(C)   If V and W are added to class 1, Z is added to class 3.
(D)   If V and X are added to class 1, W is added to class 3.
(E)   If Y and Z are added to class 2, X is added to class 2.

Exactly six employees—officers F, G, and H, and supervisors K, L, and M—must be assigned to exactly three committees—Policy, Quality, and Sales—with exactly three employees per committee. Committee assignments must conform to the following conditions:

> Each committee must have at least one officer assigned to it.
> Each employee must be assigned to at least one committee.
> All three officers must be assigned to the Policy Committee.
> G cannot be assigned to the same committee as L.
> K must be assigned to the Sales Committee.

6. Which one of the following is a group of three employees who can be assigned together to the Sales Committee?

(A)   F, G, and H
(B)   F, G, and M
(C)   G, K, and L
(D)   H, K, and L
(E)   K, L, and M

7. If H is assigned to exactly one committee, and if no committee has both F and M assigned to it, then it must be true that

(A)   G and M are both assigned to the Quality Committee
(B)   K and L are both assigned to the Sales Committee
(C)   K is assigned to exactly two committees
(D)   L is assigned to exactly two committees
(E)   M is assigned to exactly two committees

8. Which one of the following CANNOT be true?

(A)   F is assigned to exactly one committee.
(B)   G is assigned to exactly three committees.
(C)   H is assigned to exactly three committees.
(D)   K is assigned to exactly one committee.
(E)   L is assigned to exactly two committees.

9. If F is assigned to exactly three committees, and G is assigned to exactly two committees, then which one of the following must be true?

(A)   G is assigned to the Quality Committee.
(B)   G is assigned to the Sales Committee.
(C)   K is assigned to the Quality Committee.
(D)   L is assigned to the Sales Committee.
(E)   M is assigned to the Quality Committee.

10. Which one of the following is a group of three employees who can be assigned together to the Quality Committee?

(A)   F, G, and H
(B)   F, G, and K
(C)   G, H, and K
(D)   G, K, and L
(E)   H, L, and M

11. If L is assigned to exactly two committees, which one of the following must be true?

(A)   F is assigned to the Sales Committee.
(B)   G is assigned to the Sales Committee.
(C)   H is assigned to the Quality Committee.
(D)   K is assigned to the Quality Committee.
(E)   M is assigned to the Quality Committee.

12. Which one of the following CANNOT be true?

(A)   F and G are each assigned to exactly one committee.
(B)   F and H are each assigned to exactly one committee.
(C)   G and H are each assigned to exactly one committee.
(D)   F and M are both assigned to the Sales Committee.
(E)   G and K are both assigned to the Quality Committee.

Each of five students—Hubert, Lori, Paul, Regina, and Sharon—will visit exactly one of three cities—Montreal, Toronto, or Vancouver—for the month of March, according to the following conditions:

Sharon visits a different city than Paul.

Hubert visits the same city as Regina.

Lori visits Montreal or else Toronto.

If Paul visits Vancouver, Hubert visits Vancouver with him.

Each student visits one of the cities with at least one of the other four students.

1. Which one of the following could be true for March?

   (A) Hubert, Lori, and Paul visit Toronto, and Regina and Sharon visit Vancouver.
   (B) Hubert, Lori, Paul, and Regina visit Montreal, and Sharon visits Vancouver.
   (C) Hubert, Paul, and Regina visit Toronto, and Lori and Sharon visit Montreal.
   (D) Hubert, Regina, and Sharon visit Montreal, and Lori and Paul visit Vancouver.
   (E) Lori, Paul, and Sharon visit Montreal, and Hubert and Regina visit Toronto.

2. If Hubert and Sharon visit a city together, which one of the following could be true in March?

   (A) Hubert visits the same city as Paul.
   (B) Lori visits the same city as Regina.
   (C) Paul visits the same city as Regina.
   (D) Paul visits Toronto.
   (E) Paul visits Vancouver.

3. If Sharon visits Vancouver, which one of the following must be true for March?

   (A) Hubert visits Montreal.
   (B) Lori visits Montreal.
   (C) Paul visits Toronto.
   (D) Lori visits the same city as Paul.
   (E) Lori visits the same city as Regina.

4. Which one of the following could be false in March?

   (A) Sharon must visit Montreal if Paul visits Vancouver.
   (B) Regina must visit Vancouver if Paul visits Vancouver.
   (C) Regina visits a city with exactly two of the other four students.
   (D) Lori visits a city with exactly one of the other four students.
   (E) Lori visits a city with Paul or else with Sharon.

5. If Regina visits Toronto, which one of the following could be true in March?

   (A) Lori visits Toronto.
   (B) Lori visits Vancouver.
   (C) Paul visits Toronto.
   (D) Paul visits Vancouver.
   (E) Sharon visits Vancouver.

6. Which one of the following must be true for March?

   (A) If any of the students visits Montreal, Lori visits Montreal.
   (B) If any of the students visits Montreal, exactly two of them do.
   (C) If any of the students visits Toronto, exactly three of them do.
   (D) If any of the students visits Vancouver, Paul visits Vancouver.
   (E) If any of the students visits Vancouver, exactly three of them do.

Prior to this year's annual promotion review, the staff of a law firm consisted of partners Harrison and Rafael, associate Olivos, and assistants Ganz, Johnson, Lowry, Stefano, Turner, and Wilford. During each annual review, each assistant and associate is considered for promotion to the next higher rank, and at least one person is promoted from each of the two lower ranks. An assistant is promoted to associate when a majority of higher-ranking staff votes for promotion. An associate is promoted to partner when a majority of partners vote for promotion. Everyone eligible votes on every promotion. No one joins or leaves the firm.

    Olivos never votes for promoting Ganz, Johnson, or Turner.
    Rafael never votes for promoting Lowry or Stefano.
    Harrison never votes for promoting Johnson or Wilford.

20. Which one of the following could be the distribution of staff resulting from this year's review?

	Partner	Associate	Assistant
(A)	Harrison, Olivos, Rafael	Ganz, Johnson, Lowry	Stefano, Turner, Wilford
(B)	Harrison, Rafael	Lowry, Olivos, Stefano	Ganz, Johnson, Turner, Wilford
(C)	Harrison, Olivos, Rafael, Stefano	Ganz, Lowry, Turner, Wilford	Johnson
(D)	Harrison, Olivos, Rafael		Ganz, Johnson, Lowry, Stefano, Turner, Wilford
(E)	Harrison, Olivos, Rafael	Ganz, Lowry, Stefano, Turner	Johnson, Wilford,

21. If Rafael votes for promoting only Ganz, Olivos, and Wilford, and if Harrison votes for promoting only Lowry, Olivos, and Stefano, then which one of the following could be the complete roster of associates resulting from this year's review?

(A) Ganz, Lowry, Wilford
(B) Johnson, Lowry, Stefano
(C) Lowry, Stefano, Turner
(D) Lowry, Stefano, Wilford
(E) Olivos, Turner, Wilford

22. If Johnson is to be promoted to associate during next year's review, which one of the following is the smallest number of assistants who must be promoted during this year's review?

(A) one
(B) two
(C) three
(D) four
(E) five

23. Which one of the following must be true after next year's review?

(A) Lowry is an assistant.
(B) Wilford is a partner.
(C) There are no assistants.
(D) There are at least two assistants.
(E) There are no more than four assistants.

24. What is the smallest possible number of associates in the firm immediately after next year's review?

(A) none
(B) one
(C) two
(D) three
(E) four

Each of two boats, boat 1 and boat 2, will be assigned exactly four people. Exactly eight people, three adults—F, G, and H—and five children—V, W, X, Y, and Z—must be assigned to the boats according to the following conditions:

Each boat is assigned at least one adult.
If F is assigned to boat 2, G is assigned to boat 2.
If V is assigned to boat 1, W is assigned to boat 2.
X and Z are assigned to different boats.

13. Which one of the following is an acceptable assignment of people to boat 1?

    (A)   F, G, H, X
    (B)   F, H, W, Y
    (C)   F, H, Y, Z
    (D)   F, V, W, X
    (E)   G, H, X, Y

14. If F is assigned to boat 2, which one of the following is a pair of people who could be assigned to the same boat as each other?

    (A)   F and Y
    (B)   G and H
    (C)   G and Y
    (D)   V and W
    (E)   Y and Z

15. If exactly three children are assigned to boat 1, which one of the following is a pair of people who could both be assigned to boat 2?

    (A)   F and H
    (B)   G and Y
    (C)   H and W
    (D)   V and W
    (E)   W and Y

16. If G is assigned to boat 1, which one of the following must be true?

    (A)   H is assigned to boat 2.
    (B)   V is assigned to boat 2.
    (C)   Exactly one adult is assigned to boat 1.
    (D)   Exactly two adults are assigned to boat 2.
    (E)   Exactly two children are assigned to boat 2.

17. If V and W are assigned to the same boat as each other, which one of the following is a pair of people who must also be assigned to the same boat as each other?

    (A)   F and H
    (B)   F and Y
    (C)   G and X
    (D)   W and X
    (E)   Y and Z

18. If H is assigned to a different boat than Y, which one of the following must be assigned to boat 1 ?

    (A)   F
    (B)   G
    (C)   H
    (D)   V
    (E)   Y

19. If exactly one adult is assigned to boat 1, which one of the following must be true?

    (A)   F is assigned to boat 1.
    (B)   G is assigned to boat 2.
    (C)   H is assigned to boat 2.
    (D)   V is assigned to boat 1.
    (E)   Z is assigned to boat 2.

Each of nine students—Faith, Gregory, Harlan, Jennifer, Kenji, Lisa, Marcus, Nari, and Paul—will be assigned to exactly one of three panels: Oceans, Recycling, and Wetlands. Exactly three of the students will be assigned to each panel. The assignment of students to panels must meet the following conditions:

Faith is assigned to the same panel as Gregory.
Kenji is assigned to the same panel as Marcus.
Faith is not assigned to the same panel as Paul.
Gregory is not assigned to the same panel as Harlan.
Jennifer is not assigned to the same panel as Kenji.
Harlan is not assigned to the Oceans panel if Paul is not assigned to the Oceans panel.

20. Which one of the following is an acceptable assignment of students to the panels?

(A)   Oceans: Faith, Gregory, Jennifer
       Recycling: Kenji, Lisa, Nari
       Wetlands: Harlan, Marcus, Paul
(B)   Oceans: Faith, Jennifer, Lisa
       Recycling: Harlan, Kenji, Marcus
       Wetlands: Gregory, Nari, Paul
(C)   Oceans: Harlan, Kenji, Marcus
       Recycling: Faith, Gregory, Jennifer
       Wetlands: Lisa, Nari, Paul
(D)   Oceans: Jennifer, Kenji, Marcus
       Recycling: Faith, Gregory, Nari
       Wetlands: Harlan, Lisa, Paul
(E)   Oceans: Kenji, Marcus, Paul
       Recycling: Harlan, Jennifer, Nari
       Wetlands: Faith, Gregory, Lisa

21. If Marcus and Paul are both assigned to the Wetlands panel, which one of the following must be true?

(A)   Harlan is assigned to the Recycling panel.
(B)   Jennifer is assigned to the Oceans panel.
(C)   Kenji is assigned to the Recycling panel.
(D)   Lisa is assigned to the Wetlands panel.
(E)   Nari is assigned to the Oceans panel.

22. Which one of the following is a pair of students who could be assigned to the same panel as each other?

(A)   Faith and Harlan
(B)   Gregory and Paul
(C)   Harlan and Marcus
(D)   Faith and Marcus
(E)   Jennifer and Marcus

23. If Kenji and Paul are both assigned to the Recycling panel, which one of the following could be true?

(A)   Faith is assigned to the Wetlands panel.
(B)   Gregory is assigned to the Recycling panel.
(C)   Harlan is assigned to the Oceans panel.
(D)   Jennifer is assigned to the Wetlands panel.
(E)   Lisa is assigned to the Recycling panel.

24. Each of the following is a pair of students who could be assigned to the same panel as each other EXCEPT:

(A)   Gregory and Kenji
(B)   Gregory and Lisa
(C)   Kenji and Nari
(D)   Lisa and Marcus
(E)   Lisa and Paul

GROUPING

A university library budget committee must reduce exactly five of eight areas of expenditure—G, L, M, N, P, R, S, and W—in accordance with the following conditions:

If both G and S are reduced, W is also reduced.
If N is reduced, neither R nor S is reduced.
If P is reduced, L is not reduced.
Of the three areas L, M, and R, exactly two are reduced.

6. Which one of the following could be a complete and accurate list of the areas of expenditure reduced by the committee?

(A) G, L, M, N, W
(B) G, L, M, P, W
(C) G, M, N, R, W
(D) G, M, P, R, S
(E) L, M, R, S, W

7. If W is reduced, which one of the following could be a complete and accurate list of the four other areas of expenditure to be reduced?

(A) G, M, P, S
(B) L, M, N, R
(C) L, M, P, S
(D) M, N, P, S
(E) M, P, R, S

8. If P is reduced, which one of the following is a pair of areas of expenditure both of which must be reduced?

(A) G, M
(B) M, R
(C) N, R
(D) R, S
(E) S, W

9. If both L and S are reduced, which one of the following could be a pair of areas of expenditure both of which are reduced?

(A) G, M
(B) G, P
(C) N, R
(D) N, W
(E) P, S

10. If R is not reduced, which one of the following must be true?

(A) G is reduced.
(B) N is not reduced.
(C) P is reduced.
(D) S is reduced.
(E) W is not reduced.

11. If both M and R are reduced, which one of the following is a pair of areas neither of which could be reduced?

(A) G, L
(B) G, N
(C) L, N
(D) L, P
(E) P, S

12. Which one of the following areas must be reduced?

(A) G
(B) L
(C) N
(D) P
(E) W

Chapter Five:
Grouping/Linear
Combination Games

Chapter Five: Grouping/Linear Combination Games

A soloist will play six different guitar concertos, exactly one each Sunday for six consecutive weeks. Two concertos will be selected from among three concertos by Giuliani—H, J, and K; two from among four concertos by Rodrigo—M, N, O, and P; and two from among three concertos by Vivaldi—X, Y, and Z. The following conditions apply without exception:

> If N is selected, then J is also selected.
>
> If M is selected, then neither J nor O can be selected.
>
> If X is selected, then neither Z nor P can be selected.
>
> If both J and O are selected, then J is played at some time before O.
>
> X cannot be played on the fifth Sunday unless one of Rodrigo's concertos is played on the first Sunday.

19. Which one of the following is an acceptable selection of concertos that the soloist could play on the first through the sixth Sunday?

	1	2	3	4	5	6
(A)	H	Z	M	N	Y	K
(B)	K	J	Y	O	Z	N
(C)	K	Y	P	J	Z	M
(D)	P	Y	J	H	X	O
(E)	X	N	K	O	J	Z

20. If the six concertos to be played are J, K, N, O, Y, and Z and if N is to be played on the first Sunday, then which one of the following concertos CANNOT be played on the second Sunday?

(A) J
(B) K
(C) O
(D) Y
(E) Z

21. If J, O, and Y are the first three concertos to be played, not necessarily in the order given, which one of the following is a concerto that CANNOT be played on the fifth Sunday?

(A) H
(B) K
(C) N
(D) P
(E) X

22. If O is selected for the first Sunday, which one of the following is a concerto that must also be selected?

(A) J
(B) K
(C) M
(D) N
(E) X

23. Which one of the following is a concerto that must be selected?

(A) J
(B) K
(C) O
(D) Y
(E) Z

24. Which one of the following is a concerto that CANNOT be selected together with N?

(A) M
(B) O
(C) P
(D) X
(E) Z

An art teacher will schedule exactly six of eight lectures—fresco, history, lithography, naturalism, oils, pastels, sculpture, and watercolors—for three days—1, 2, and 3. There will be exactly two lectures each day—morning and afternoon. Scheduling is governed by the following conditions:

    Day 2 is the only day for which oils can be scheduled.

    Neither sculpture nor watercolors can be scheduled for the afternoon.

    Neither oils nor pastels can be scheduled for the same day as lithography.

    If pastels is scheduled for day 1 or day 2, then the lectures scheduled for the day immediately following pastels must be fresco and history, not necessarily in that order.

12. Which one of the following is an acceptable schedule of lectures for days 1, 2, and 3, respectively?

  (A)   Morning: lithography, history, sculpture
          Afternoon: pastels, fresco, naturalism
  (B)   Morning: naturalism, oils, fresco
          Afternoon: lithography, pastels, history
  (C)   Morning: oils, history, naturalism
          Afternoon: pastels, fresco, lithography
  (D)   Morning: sculpture, lithography, naturalism
          Afternoon: watercolors, fresco, pastels
  (E)   Morning: sculpture, pastels, fresco
          Afternoon: lithography, history, naturalism

13. If lithography and fresco are scheduled for the afternoons of day 2 and day 3, respectively, which one of the following is a lecture that could be scheduled for the afternoon of day 1?

  (A)   history
  (B)   oils
  (C)   pastels
  (D)   sculpture
  (E)   watercolors

14. If lithography and history are scheduled for the mornings of day 2 and day 3, respectively, which one of the following lectures could be scheduled for the morning of day 1?

  (A)   fresco
  (B)   naturalism
  (C)   oils
  (D)   pastels
  (E)   sculpture

15. If oils and lithography are scheduled for the mornings of day 2 and day 3, respectively, which one of the following CANNOT be scheduled for any day?

  (A)   fresco
  (B)   history
  (C)   naturalism
  (D)   pastels
  (E)   sculpture

16. If neither fresco nor naturalism is scheduled for any day, which one of the following must be scheduled for day 1?

  (A)   history
  (B)   lithography
  (C)   oils
  (D)   pastels
  (E)   sculpture

17. If the lectures scheduled for the mornings are fresco, history, and lithography, not necessarily in that order, which one of the following could be true?

  (A)   Lithography is scheduled for day 3.
  (B)   Naturalism is scheduled for day 2.
  (C)   Fresco is scheduled for the same day as naturalism.
  (D)   History is scheduled for the same day as naturalism.
  (E)   History is scheduled for the same day as oils.

At an evening concert, a total of six songs—O, P, T, X, Y, and Z—will be performed by three vocalists—George, Helen, and Leslie. The songs will be sung consecutively as solos, and each will be performed exactly once. The following constraints govern the composition of the concert program:

Y must be performed earlier than T and earlier than O.

P must be performed earlier than Z and later than O.

George can perform only X, Y, and Z. Helen can perform only T, P, and X.

Leslie can perform only O, P, and X.

The vocalist who performs first must be different from the vocalist who performs last.

19. Which one of the following is an acceptable schedule for the performance of the songs, in order from the first to last song performed?

    (A) X, T, Y, O, P, Z
    (B) X, Z, Y, T, O, P
    (C) Y, O, P, X, T, Z
    (D) Y, P, O, Z, T, X
    (E) Y, X, O, P, Z, T

20. Which one of the following must be true about the program?

    (A) George performs X.
    (B) Helen performs O.
    (C) Helen performs T.
    (D) Leslie performs P.
    (E) Leslie performs X.

21. Which one of the following is a complete and accurate list of the songs any one of which could be the last song performed at the concert?

    (A) O, P, Z
    (B) O, T, X
    (C) T, P, Z
    (D) T, X, Z
    (E) X, P, Z

22. If X is performed first, which one of the following must be true?

    (A) X is performed by George.
    (B) X is performed by Helen.
    (C) P is the fourth song performed.
    (D) Y is the second song performed.
    (E) Y is the third song performed.

23. Each of the following is an acceptable schedule for the performance of the songs, in order from the first to last song performed, EXCEPT:

    (A) Y, O, P, T, Z, X
    (B) Y, T, O, P, X, Z
    (C) Y, X, O, P, Z, T
    (D) X, Y, O, P, Z, T
    (E) X, Y, O, T, P, Z

24. If Y is performed first, the songs performed second, third, and fourth, respectively, could be

    (A) T, X, and O
    (B) T, Z, and O
    (C) X, O, and P
    (D) X, P, and Z
    (E) X, T, and O

Chapter Six:
Pure Sequencing Games

Chapter Six: Pure Sequencing Games

The eight partners of a law firm are Gregg, Hodges, Ivan, James, King, MacNeil, Nader, and Owens. In each of the years 1961 through 1968, exactly one of the partners joined the firm.

Hodges joined the firm before Nader.
King joined the firm before James.
Nader and James joined the firm before Gregg.
Nader joined the firm before Owens.
James joined the firm before MacNeil.
Gregg joined the firm before Ivan.

14. Which one of the following CANNOT be true?

(A) Hodges joined the law firm in 1961.
(B) Hodges joined the law firm in 1963.
(C) Gregg joined the law firm in 1964.
(D) MacNeil joined the law firm in 1964.
(E) Owens joined the law firm in 1964.

15. If James joined the firm in 1962, which one of the following CANNOT be true?

(A) Hodges joined the firm in 1963.
(B) MacNeil joined the firm in 1963.
(C) Hodges joined the firm in 1964.
(D) Nader joined the firm in 1964.
(E) Owens joined the firm in 1964.

16. Of the following, which one is the latest year in which James could have joined the firm?

(A) 1962
(B) 1963
(C) 1964
(D) 1965
(E) 1966

17. If Owens joined the firm in 1965 and MacNeil joined it in 1967, one can determine the years in which exactly how many of the other partners joined the firm?

(A) 1
(B) 2
(C) 3
(D) 4
(E) 5

18. Assume that Owens joined the law firm before MacNeil. Of the following, which one is the earliest year in which MacNeil could have joined it?

(A) 1963
(B) 1964
(C) 1965
(D) 1966
(E) 1967

The Mammoth Corporation has just completed hiring nine new workers: Brandt, Calva, Duvall, Eberle, Fu, Garcia, Haga, Irving, and Jessup.

> Fu and Irving were hired on the same day as each other, and no one else was hired that day.
> Calva and Garcia were hired on the same day as each other, and no one else was hired that day.
> On each of the other days of hiring, exactly one worker was hired.
> Eberle was hired before Brandt.
> Haga was hired before Duvall.
> Duvall was hired after Irving but before Eberle.
> Garcia was hired after both Jessup and Brandt.
> Brandt was hired before Jessup.

1. Who were the last two workers to be hired?

   (A) Eberle and Jessup
   (B) Brandt and Garcia
   (C) Brandt and Calva
   (D) Garcia and Calva
   (E) Jessup and Brandt

2. Who was hired on the fourth day of hiring?

   (A) Eberle
   (B) Brandt
   (C) Irving
   (D) Garcia
   (E) Jessup

3. Exactly how many workers were hired before Jessup?

   (A) 6
   (B) 5
   (C) 4
   (D) 3
   (E) 2

4. Which one of the following must be true?

   (A) Duvall was the first worker to be hired.
   (B) Haga was the first worker to be hired.
   (C) Fu and Irving were the first two workers to be hired.
   (D) Haga and Fu were the first two workers to be hired.
   (E) Either Haga was the first worker to be hired or Fu and Irving were the first two workers to be hired.

5. If Eberle was hired on a Monday, what is the earliest day on which Garcia could have been hired?

   (A) Monday
   (B) Tuesday
   (C) Wednesday
   (D) Thursday
   (E) Friday

A law firm has exactly nine partners: Fox, Glassen, Hae, Inman, Jacoby, Kohn, Lopez, Malloy, and Nassar.

Kohn's salary is greater than both Inman's and Lopez's.

Lopez's salary is greater than Nassar's.

Inman's salary is greater than Fox's.

Fox's salary is greater than Malloy's.

Malloy's salary is greater than Glassen's.

Glassen's salary is greater than Jacoby's.

Jacoby's salary is greater than Hae's.

1. Which one of the following partners cannot have the third highest salary?

    (A)   Fox
    (B)   Inman
    (C)   Lopez
    (D)   Malloy
    (E)   Nassar

2. If Malloy and Nassar earn the same salary, at least how many of the partners must have lower salaries than Lopez?

    (A)   3
    (B)   4
    (C)   5
    (D)   6
    (E)   7

3. The salary rankings of each of the nine partners could be completely determined if which one of the following statements were true?

    (A)   Lopez's salary is greater than Fox's.
    (B)   Lopez's salary is greater than Inman's.
    (C)   Nassar's salary is greater than Fox's.
    (D)   Nassar's salary is greater than Inman's.
    (E)   Nassar's salary is greater than Malloy's.

4. If Nassar's salary is the same as that of one other partner of the firm, which one of the following must be false?

    (A)   Inman's salary is less than Lopez's.
    (B)   Jacoby's salary is less than Lopez's.
    (C)   Lopez's salary is less than Fox's.
    (D)   Lopez's salary is less than Hae's.
    (E)   Nassar's salary is less than Glassen's.

5. What is the minimum number of different salaries earned by the nine partners of the firm?

    (A)   5
    (B)   6
    (C)   7
    (D)   8
    (E)   9

6. Assume that the partners of the firm are ranked according to their salaries, from first (highest) to ninth (lowest), and that no two salaries are the same. Which one of the following is a complete and accurate list of Glassen's possible ranks?

    (A)   fifth
    (B)   fifth, sixth
    (C)   fifth, seventh
    (D)   fifth, sixth, seventh
    (E)   fifth, sixth, seventh, eighth

A soft drink manufacturer surveyed consumer preferences for exactly seven proposed names for its new soda: Jazz, Kola, Luck, Mist, Nipi, Oboy, and Ping. The manufacturer ranked the seven names according to the number of votes they received. The name that received the most votes was ranked first. Every name received a different number of votes. Some of the survey results are as follows:

Jazz received more votes than Oboy.
Oboy received more votes than Kola.
Kola received more votes than Mist.
Nipi did not receive the fewest votes.
Ping received fewer votes than Luck but more votes than Nipi and more votes than Oboy.

7. Which one of the following could be an accurate list of the seven names in rank order from first through seventh?

   (A)   Jazz, Luck, Ping, Nipi, Kola, Oboy, Mist
   (B)   Jazz, Luck, Ping, Oboy, Kola, Mist, Nipi
   (C)   Luck, Ping, Jazz, Nipi, Oboy, Kola, Mist
   (D)   Luck, Ping, Nipi, Oboy, Jazz, Kola, Mist
   (E)   Ping, Luck, Jazz, Oboy, Nipi, Kola, Mist

8. Which one of the following statements must be true?

   (A)   Jazz received more votes than Nipi.
   (B)   Kola received more votes than Nipi.
   (C)   Luck received more votes than Jazz.
   (D)   Nipi received more votes than Oboy.
   (E)   Ping received more votes than Kola.

9. If the ranks of Ping, Oboy, and Kola were consecutive, then which one of the following statements would have to be false?

   (A)   Jazz received more votes than Luck.
   (B)   Jazz received more votes than Ping.
   (C)   Nipi received more votes than Oboy.
   (D)   Nipi received more votes than Mist.
   (E)   Oboy received more votes than Nipi.

10. What is the total number of the soft drink names whose exact ranks can be deduced from the partial survey results?

   (A)   one
   (B)   two
   (C)   three
   (D)   four
   (E)   five

11. What is the maximum possible number of the soft drink names any one of which could be among the three most popular?

   (A)   three
   (B)   four
   (C)   five
   (D)   six
   (E)   seven

12. If Ping received more votes than Jazz, then what is the maximum possible number of names whose ranks can be determined?

   (A)   two
   (B)   three
   (C)   four
   (D)   five
   (E)   six

On the basis of an examination, nine students—Fred, Glen, Hilary, Ida, Jan, Kathy, Laura, Mike, and Nick—are each placed in one of three classes. The three highest scorers are placed in the level 1 class; the three lowest scorers are placed in the level 3 class. The remaining three are placed in the level 2 class. Each class has exactly three students.

> Ida scores higher than Glen.
> Glen scores higher than both Jan and Kathy.
> Jan scores higher than Mike.
> Mike scores higher than Hilary.
> Hilary scores higher than Nick.
> Kathy scores higher than both Fred and Laura.

1. How many different combinations of students could form the level 1 class?

    (A) one
    (B) two
    (C) three
    (D) four
    (E) six

2. Which one of the following students could be in the level 2 class but cannot be in the level 3 class?

    (A) Fred
    (B) Glen
    (C) Jan
    (D) Kathy
    (E) Nick

3. Which one of the following students could be placed in any one of the three classes?

    (A) Fred
    (B) Jan
    (C) Kathy
    (D) Laura
    (E) Mike

4. The composition of each class can be completely determined if which one of the following pairs of students is known to be in the level 2 class?

    (A) Fred and Kathy
    (B) Fred and Mike
    (C) Hilary and Jan
    (D) Kathy and Laura
    (E) Laura and Mike

5. Which one of the following pairs of students cannot be in the same class as Fred?

    (A) Hilary and Nick
    (B) Jan and Laura
    (C) Kathy and Laura
    (D) Jan and Mike
    (E) Laura and Mike

Chapter Seven:
The Forgotten Few

Chapter Seven: The Forgotten Few

Three boys—Karl, Luis, and Miguel—and three girls—
Rita, Sarah, and Tura—are giving a dance recital.
Three dances—1, 2, and 3—are to be performed. Each
dance involves three pairs of children, a boy and a girl
partnering each other in each pair, according to the
following conditions:

Karl partners Sarah in either dance 1 or dance 2.
Whoever partners Rita in dance 2 must partner
Sarah in dance 3.
No two children can partner each other in more
than one dance.

14. If Sarah partners Luis in dance 3, which one of the
following is a complete and accurate list of the girls
any one of whom could partner Miguel in dance 1?

(A) Rita
(B) Sarah
(C) Tura
(D) Rita, Sarah
(E) Rita, Tura

15. If Miguel partners Rita in dance 2, which one of
the following could be true?

(A) Karl partners Tura in dance 1.
(B) Luis partners Sarah in dance 2.
(C) Luis partners Sarah in dance 3.
(D) Miguel partners Sarah in dance 1.
(E) Miguel partners Tura in dance 3.

16. If Miguel partners Sarah in dance 1, which one of
the following is a pair of children who must partner
each other in dance 3?

(A) Karl and Rita
(B) Karl and Tura
(C) Luis and Rita
(D) Luis and Tura
(E) Miguel and Tura

17. If Luis partners Sarah in dance 2, which one of the
following is a pair of children who must partner
each other in dance 1?

(A) Karl and Rita
(B) Karl and Tura
(C) Luis and Rita
(D) Luis and Tura
(E) Miguel and Rita

18. If Miguel partners Rita in dance 1, which one of
the following must be true?

(A) Karl partners Rita in dance 2.
(B) Karl partners Sarah in dance 3.
(C) Karl partners Tura in dance 1.
(D) Luis partners Rita in dance 2.
(E) Luis partners Tura in dance 3.

In a game, "words" (real or nonsensical) consist of any combination of at least four letters of the English alphabet. Any "sentence" consists of exactly five words and satisfies the following conditions:

The five words are written from left to right on a single line in alphabetical order.

The sentence is started by any word, and each successive word is formed by applying exactly one of three operations to the word immediately to its left: delete one letter; add one letter; replace one letter with another letter.

At most three of the five words begin with the same letter as one another.

Except for the leftmost word, each word is formed by a different operation from that which formed the word immediately to its left.

13. Which one of the following could be a sentence in the word game?

(A)	bzeak	bleak	leak	peak	pea
(B)	crbek	creek	reek	seek	sxeek
(C)	dteam	gleam	glean	lean	mean
(D)	feed	freed	reed	seed	seeg
(E)	food	fool	fools	fopls	opls

14. The last letter of the alphabet that the first word of a sentence in the word game can begin with is

(A) t
(B) w
(C) x
(D) y
(E) z

15. If the first word in a sentence is "blender" and the third word is "slender," then the second word can be

(A) bender
(B) gender
(C) lender
(D) sender
(E) tender

16. If the first word in a sentence consists of nine letters, then the minimum number of letters that the fourth word can contain is

(A) four
(B) five
(C) six
(D) seven
(E) eight

17. If "clean" is the first word in a sentence and "learn" is another word in the sentence, then which one of the following is a complete and accurate list of the positions each of which could be the position in which "learn" occurs in the sentence?

(A) second
(B) third
(C) fourth, fifth
(D) second, third, fourth
(E) third, fourth, fifth

18. If the first word in a sentence consists of four letters, then the maximum number of letters that the fifth word in this sentence could contain is

(A) four
(B) five
(C) six
(D) seven
(E) eight

The population of a small country is organized into five clans—N, O, P, S, and T. Each year exactly three of the five clans participate in the annual harvest ceremonies. The rules specifying the order of participation of the clans in the ceremonies are as follows:

Each clan must participate at least once in any two consecutive years.

No clan participates for three consecutive years.

Participation takes place in cycles, with each cycle ending when each of the five clans has participated three times. Only then does a new cycle begin.

No clan participates more than three times within any cycle.

18. If the clans participating in the first year of a given cycle are N, O, and P, which one of the following could be the clans participating in the second year of that cycle?

(A) N, O, S
(B) N, O, T
(C) N, P, S
(D) O, P, T
(E) O, S, T

19. Which one of the following can be true about the clans' participation in the ceremonies?

(A) N participates in the first, second, and third years.
(B) N participates in the second, third, and fourth years.
(C) Both O and S participate in the first and third years.
(D) Both N and S participate in the first, third, and fifth years.
(E) Both S and T participate in the second, third, and fifth years.

20. Any cycle for the clans' participation in the ceremonies must be completed at the end of exactly how many years?

(A) five
(B) six
(C) seven
(D) eight
(E) nine

21. Which one of the following must be true about the three clans that participate in the ceremonies in the first year?

(A) At most two of them participate together in the third year.
(B) At least two of them participate together in the second year.
(C) All three of them participate together in the fourth year.
(D) All three of them participate together in the fifth year.
(E) None of them participates in the third year.

22. If, in a particular cycle, N, O, and S participate in the ceremonies in the first year, which one of the following must be true?

(A) N participates in the second and third years.
(B) O participates in the third and fourth years.
(C) N and O both participate in the third year.
(D) P and T both participate in the fifth year.
(E) S and T both participate in the fifth year.

23. If, in a particular cycle, N, O, and T participate in the first year and if O and P participate in the fourth year, any of the following could be a clan that participates in the third year EXCEPT

(A) N
(B) O
(C) P
(D) S
(E) T

24. If, in a particular cycle, N, O, and S participate in the ceremonies in the first year and O, S, and T participate in the third year, then which one of the following could be the clans that participate in the fifth year?

(A) N, O, P
(B) N, O, S
(C) N, P, S
(D) O, P, S
(E) P, S, T

Within a tennis league each of five teams occupies one of five positions, numbered 1 through 5 in order of rank, with number 1 as the highest position. The teams are initially in the order R, J, S, M, L, with R in position 1. Teams change positions only when a lower-positioned team defeats a higher-positioned team. The rules are as follows:

    Matches are played alternately in odd-position rounds and in even-position rounds.

    In an odd-position round, teams in positions 3 and 5 play against teams positioned immediately above them.

    In an even-position round, teams in positions 2 and 4 play against teams positioned immediately above them.

    When a lower-positioned team defeats a higher-positioned team, the two teams switch positions after the round is completed.

19. Which one of the following could be the order of teams, from position 1 through position 5 respectively, after exactly one round of even-position matches if no odd-position round has yet been played?

    (A)   J, R, M, L, S
    (B)   J, R, S, L, M
    (C)   R, J, M, L, S
    (D)   R, J, M, S, L
    (E)   R, S, J, L, M

20. If exactly two rounds of matches have been played, beginning with an odd-position round, and if the lower-positioned teams have won every match in those two rounds, then each of the following must be true EXCEPT:

    (A)   L is one position higher than J.
    (B)   R is one position higher than L.
    (C)   S is one position higher than R.
    (D)   J is in position 4.
    (E)   M is in position 3.

21. Which one of the following could be true after exactly two rounds of matches have been played?

    (A)   J has won two matches.
    (B)   L has lost two matches.
    (C)   R has won two matches.
    (D)   L's only match was played against J.
    (E)   M played against S in two matches.

22. If after exactly three rounds of matches M is in position 4, and J and L have won all of their matches, then which one of the following can be true?

    (A)   J is in position 2.
    (B)   J is in position 3.
    (C)   L is in position 2.
    (D)   R is in position 1.
    (E)   S is in position 3.

23. If after exactly three rounds M has won three matches and the rankings of the other four teams relative to each other remain the same, then which one of the following must be in position 3?

    (A)   J
    (B)   L
    (C)   M
    (D)   R
    (E)   S

24. If after exactly three rounds the teams, in order from first to fifth position, are R, J, L, S, and M, then which one of the following could be the order, from first to fifth position, of the teams after the second round?

    (A)   J, R, M, S, L
    (B)   J, L, S, M, R
    (C)   R, J, S, L, M
    (D)   R, L, M, S, J
    (E)   R, M, L, S, J

A jeweler makes a single strand of beads by threading onto a string in a single direction from a clasp a series of solid colored beads. Each bead is either green, orange, purple, red, or yellow. The resulting strand satisfies the following specifications:

If a purple bead is adjacent to a yellow bead, any bead that immediately follows and any bead that immediately precedes that pair must be red.

Any pair of beads adjacent to each other that are the same color as each other must be green.

No orange bead can be adjacent to any red bead.

Any portion of the strand containing eight consecutive beads must include at least one bead of each color.

13. If the strand has exactly eight beads, which one of the following is an acceptable order, starting from the clasp, for the eight beads?

   (A) green, red, purple, yellow, red, orange, green, purple
   (B) orange, yellow, red, red, yellow, purple, red, green
   (C) purple, yellow, red, green, green, orange, yellow, orange
   (D) red, orange, red, yellow, purple, green, yellow, green
   (E) red, yellow, purple, red, green, red, green, green

14. If an orange bead is the fourth bead from the clasp, which one of the following is a pair that could be the second and third beads, respectively?

   (A) green, orange
   (B) green, red
   (C) purple, purple
   (D) yellow, green
   (E) yellow, purple

15. If on an eight bead strand the second, third, and fourth beads from the clasp are red, green, and yellow, respectively, and the sixth and seventh beads are purple and red, respectively, then which one of the following must be true?

   (A) The first bead is purple.
   (B) The fifth bead is green.
   (C) The fifth bead is orange.
   (D) The eighth bead is orange.
   (E) The eighth bead is yellow.

16. If on a six-bead strand the first and second beads from the clasp are purple and yellow, respectively, then the fifth and sixth beads CANNOT be

   (A) green and orange, respectively
   (B) orange and green, respectively
   (C) orange and yellow, respectively
   (D) purple and orange, respectively
   (E) yellow and purple, respectively

17. If on a nine-bead strand the first and fourth beads from the clasp are purple, and the second and fifth beads are yellow, which one of the following could be true?

   (A) The seventh bead is orange.
   (B) The eighth bead is green.
   (C) The eighth bead is red.
   (D) The ninth bead is red.
   (E) The ninth bead is yellow.

18. If on an eight-bead strand the first, second, third, and fourth beads from the clasp are red, yellow, green, and red, respectively, then the fifth and sixth beads CANNOT be

   (A) green and orange, respectively
   (B) green and purple, respectively
   (C) purple and orange, respectively
   (D) purple and yellow, respectively
   (E) yellow and orange, respectively

Game #6: June 1991 Questions 1-7

Exactly six trade representatives negotiate a treaty: Klosnik, Londi, Manley, Neri, Osata, Poirier. There are exactly six chairs evenly spaced around a circular table. The chairs are numbered 1 through 6, with successively numbered chairs next to each other and chair number 1 next to chair number 6. Each chair is occupied by exactly one of the representatives. The following conditions apply:

Poirier sits immediately next to Neri.
Londi sits immediately next to Manley, Neri, or both.
Klosnik does not sit immediately next to Manley.
If Osata sits immediately next to Poirier, Osata does not sit immediately next to Manley.

1. Which one of the following seating arrangements of the six representatives in chairs 1 through 6 would NOT violate the stated conditions?

    (A)   Klosnik, Poirier, Neri, Manley, Osata, Londi
    (B)   Klosnik, Londi, Manley, Poirier, Neri, Osata
    (C)   Klosnik, Londi, Manley, Osata, Poirier, Neri
    (D)   Klosnik, Osata, Poirier, Neri, Londi, Manley
    (E)   Klosnik, Neri, Londi, Osata, Manley, Poirier

2. If Londi sits immediately next to Poirier, which one of the following is a pair of representatives who must sit immediately next to each other?

    (A)   Klosnik and Osata
    (B)   Londi and Neri
    (C)   Londi and Osata
    (D)   Manley and Neri
    (E)   Manley and Poirier

3. If Klosnik sits directly between Londi and Poirier, then Manley must sit directly between

    (A)   Londi and Neri
    (B)   Londi and Osata
    (C)   Neri and Osata
    (D)   Neri and Poirier
    (E)   Osata and Poirier

4. If Neri sits immediately next to Manley, then Klosnik can sit directly between

    (A)   Londi and Manley
    (B)   Londi and Poirier
    (C)   Neri and Osata
    (D)   Neri and Poirier
    (E)   Poirier and Osata

5. If Londi sits immediately next to Manley, then which one of the following is a complete and accurate list of representatives any one of whom could also sit immediately next to Londi?

    (A)   Klosnik
    (B)   Klosnik, Neri
    (C)   Neri, Poirier
    (D)   Klosnik, Osata, Poirier
    (E)   Klosnik, Neri, Osata, Poirier

6. If Londi sits immediately next to Neri, which one of the following statements must be false?

    (A)   Klosnik sits immediately next to Osata.
    (B)   Londi sits immediately next to Manley.
    (C)   Osata sits immediately next to Poirier.
    (D)   Neri sits directly between Londi and Poirier.
    (E)   Osata sits directly between Klosnik and Manley.

7. If Klosnik sits immediately next to Osata, then Londi CANNOT sit directly between

    (A)   Klosnik and Manley
    (B)   Klosnik and Neri
    (C)   Manley and Neri
    (D)   Manley and Poirier
    (E)   Neri and Osata

Eight benches—J, K, L, T, U, X, Y, and Z—are arranged along the perimeter of a park as shown below:

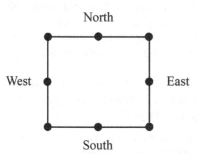

North

West   East

South

The following is true:
    J, K, and L are green; T and U are red; X, Y, and Z are pink.
    The green benches stand next to one another along the park's perimeter.
    The pink benches stand next to one another along the park's perimeter.
    No green bench stands next to a pink bench.
    The bench on the southeast corner is T.
    J stands at the center of the park's north side.
    If T stands next to X, then T does not also stand next to L.

13. Which one of the following benches could be on the northeast corner of the park?

    (A)   Z
    (B)   Y
    (C)   X
    (D)   T
    (E)   L

14. Each of the following statements must be true EXCEPT:

    (A)   The bench on the northwest corner is pink.
    (B)   The bench on the northeast corner is green.
    (C)   The bench on the southwest corner is pink.
    (D)   The middle bench on the east side of the park is green.
    (E)   The middle bench on the west side of the park is pink.

15. Which one of the following benches must be next to J?

    (A)   K
    (B)   L
    (C)   T
    (D)   U
    (E)   X

16. For which one of the following benches are there two and no more than two locations either one of which could be the location the bench occupies?

    (A)   K
    (B)   T
    (C)   X
    (D)   Y
    (E)   Z

17. If Z is directly north of Y, which one of the following statements must be true?

    (A)   J is directly west of K.
    (B)   K is directly east of U.
    (C)   U is directly north of X.
    (D)   X is directly south of J.
    (E)   Z is directly south of J.

18. If Y is in the middle of the west side of the park, then the two benches in which one of the following pairs CANNOT be two of the corner benches?

    (A)   K and X
    (B)   K and Z
    (C)   L and U
    (D)   L and X
    (E)   L and Z

19. If Y is farther south than L and farther north than T, then the benches in each of the following pairs must be next to each other EXCEPT

    (A)   J and L
    (B)   K and T
    (C)   T and X
    (D)   U and Y
    (E)   X and Z

A lake contains exactly five islands—J, K, L, M, O—which are unconnected by bridges. Contractors will build a network of bridges that satisfies the following specifications:

> Each bridge directly connects exactly two islands with each other, and no two bridges intersect.
> No more than one bridge directly connects any two islands.
> No island has more than three bridges that directly connect it with other islands.
> J, K, and L are each directly connected by bridge with one or both of M and O.
> J is directly connected by bridge with exactly two islands.
> K is directly connected by bridge with exactly one island.
> A bridge directly connects J with O, and a bridge directly connects M with O.

20. Which one of the following is a complete and accurate list of the islands any one of which could be directly connected by bridge with L?

    (A) J, K
    (B) J, M
    (C) J, O
    (D) J, M, O
    (E) J, K, M, O

21. Which one of the following could be true about the completed network of bridges?

    (A) J is directly connected by bridge both with L and with M.
    (B) K is directly connected by bridge both with M and with O.
    (C) L is directly connected by bridge both with J and with M.
    (D) M is directly connected by bridge with J, with K, and with L.
    (E) O is directly connected by bridge with K, with L, and with M.

22. If a bridge directly connects K with O, then which one of the following could be true?

    (A) No bridge directly connects L with M.
    (B) A bridge directly connects J with L.
    (C) A bridge directly connects L with O.
    (D) There are exactly three bridges directly connecting L with other islands.
    (E) There are exactly two bridges directly connecting O with other islands.

23. If a bridge directly connects L with M and a bridge directly connects L with O, then which one of the following must be true?

    (A) A bridge directly connects J with M.
    (B) A bridge directly connects K with M.
    (C) A bridge directly connects K with O.
    (D) There are exactly two bridges directly connecting L with other islands.
    (E) There are exactly two bridges directly connecting M with other islands.

24. If no island that is directly connected by bridge with M is also directly connected by bridge with O, then there must be a bridge directly connecting

    (A) J with L
    (B) J with M
    (C) K with O
    (D) L with M
    (E) L with O

Six cities are located within the numbered areas as follows:

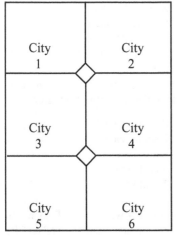

Within the six-city area there are exactly four hospitals, two jails, and two universities. These eight institutions are located as follows:

No institution is in more than one of the cities.
None of the cities contains more than one jail, and none contains more than one university.
None of the cities contains both a jail and a university.
Each jail is located in a city that contains at least one hospital.
The universities are located in two cities that do not share a common boundary.
City 3 contains a university, and city 6 contains a jail.

19. Which one of the following could be true?

(A) City 5 contains a university.
(B) City 6 contains a university.
(C) City 2 contains a jail.
(D) City 3 contains a jail.
(E) City 3 contains a hospital.

20. Which one of the following could be true?

(A) City 1 contains exactly one hospital.
(B) City 1 contains exactly one university.
(C) City 2 contains exactly one jail.
(D) City 5 contains exactly one university.
(E) City 6 contains exactly one university.

21. Which one of the following is a complete and accurate list of the cities any one of which could contain the jail that is not in city 6?

(A) 1, 4
(B) 2, 4
(C) 4, 5
(D) 1, 4, 5
(E) 1, 2, 4, 5

22. If each of the six cities contains at least one of the eight institutions, then which one of the following must be true?

(A) There is a jail in city 1.
(B) There is a hospital in city 2.
(C) There is a hospital in city 3.
(D) There is a hospital in city 4.
(E) There is a jail in city 4.

23. In which one of the following cities must there be fewer than three hospitals?

(A) 1
(B) 2
(C) 4
(D) 5
(E) 6

24. If one of the cities contains exactly two hospitals and exactly one university, then which one of the following lists three cities that might, among them, contain no hospital?

(A) 1, 3, 5
(B) 1, 4, 5
(C) 2, 3, 5
(D) 2, 4, 6
(E) 4, 5, 6

The country of Zendu contains exactly four areas for radar detection: R, S, T, and U. Each detection area is circular and falls completely within Zendu. Part of R intersects T; part of S also intersects T; R does not intersect S. Area U is completely within R and also completely within T. At noon exactly four planes—J, K, L, M—are over Zendu, in a manner consistent with the following statements:

Each plane is in at least one of the four areas.
J is in area S.
K is not in any detection area that J is in.
L is not in any detection area that M is in.
M is in exactly one of the areas.

7. Which one of the following could be a complete listing of the planes located in the four areas at noon, with each plane listed in every area in which it is located?

   (A) R: J, L;   S: J, M;   T: L;   U: L
   (B) R: J, L;   S: K;   T: M;   U: none
   (C) R: K;   S: J;   T: L;   U: M
   (D) R: K, M;   S: J, L;   T: J;   U: none
   (E) R: M;   S: J, K;   T: J, L; U: none

8. If at noon K is within exactly two of the four areas, then which one of the following CANNOT be true at that time?

   (A) J is within area T.
   (B) K is within area R.
   (C) K is within area T.
   (D) L is within area R.
   (E) L is within area T.

9. Which one of the following is a complete and accurate list of those planes any one of which could be within area T at noon?

   (A) M
   (B) J, L
   (C) J, L, M
   (D) K, L, M
   (E) J, K, L, M

10. Which one of the following statements CANNOT be true at noon about the planes?

   (A) K is within area T.
   (B) K is within area U.
   (C) L is within area R.
   (D) M is within area R.
   (E) M is within area U.

11. It CANNOT be true that at noon there is at least one plane that is within both area

   (A) R and area T
   (B) R and area U
   (C) S and area T
   (D) S and area U
   (E) T and area U

12. If at noon M is within area T, then which one of the following statements CANNOT be true at that time?

   (A) J is within area T.
   (B) L is within area R.
   (C) L is within area S.
   (D) K is within exactly two areas.
   (E) L is within exactly two areas.

13. If at noon plane L is within exactly three of the areas, which one of the following could be true at that time?

   (A) J is within exactly two of the areas.
   (B) J is within exactly three of the areas.
   (C) K is within area S.
   (D) M is within area R.
   (E) M is within area T.

Greenburg has exactly five subway lines: L1, L2, L3, L4, and L5. Along each of the lines, trains run in both directions, stopping at every station.

L1 runs in a loop connecting exactly seven stations, their order being Rincon-Tonka-French-Semplain-Urstine-Quetzal-Park-Rincon in one direction of travel, and the reverse in the other direction.

L2 connects Tonka with Semplain, and with no other station.

L3 connects Rincon with Urstine, and with no other station.

L4 runs from Quetzal through exactly one other station, Greene, to Rincon.

L5 connects Quetzal with Tonka, and with no other station.

14. How many different stations are there that a traveler starting at Rincon could reach by using the subway lines without making any intermediate stops?

(A) two
(B) three
(C) four
(D) five
(E) six

15. In order to go from Greene to Semplain taking the fewest possible subway lines and making the fewest possible stops, a traveler must make a stop at

(A) French
(B) Park
(C) Quetzal
(D) Rincon
(E) Tonka

16. If L3 is not running and a traveler goes by subway from Urstine to Rincon making the fewest possible stops, which one of the following lists all of the intermediate stations in sequence along one of the routes that the traveler could take?

(A) Quetzal, Tonka
(B) Semplain, French
(C) Semplain, Park
(D) Quetzal, Park, Greene
(E) Semplain, French, Tonka

17. In order to go by subway from French to Greene, the minimum number of intermediate stops a traveler must make is

(A) zero
(B) one
(C) two
(D) three
(E) four

18. If the tracks that directly connect Urstine and Quetzal are blocked in both directions, a traveler going from Semplain to Park and making the fewest possible intermediate stops must pass through

(A) French or Tonka
(B) Greene or Urstine
(C) Quetzal or Tonka
(D) Quetzal or Urstine or both
(E) Rincon or Tonka or both

19. If a sixth subway line is to be constructed so that all of the stations would have two or more lines reaching them, the stations connected by the new subway line must include at least

(A) French, Greene, and Park
(B) French, Greene, and Quetzal
(C) French, Greene, and Rincon
(D) Park, Tonka, and Urstine
(E) Park, Semplain, and Tonka

Chapter Eight:
Advanced Features and Techniques Games

Chapter Eight: Advanced Features and Techniques Games

Hannah spends 14 days, exclusive of travel time, in a total of six cities.

Each city she visits is in one of three countries—X, Y, or Z.

Each of the three countries has many cities.

Hannah visits at least one city in each of the three countries.

She spends at least two days in each city she visits.

She spends only whole days in any city.

13. If Hannah spends exactly eight days in the cities of country X, then which one of the following CANNOT be true?

(A) She visits exactly two cities in country X.
(B) She visits exactly two cities in country Y.
(C) She visits exactly two cities in country Z.
(D) She visits more cities in country Y than in country Z.
(E) She visits more cities in country Z than in country Y.

14. If Hannah visits an equal number of cities in each of the countries, what is the greatest total number of days she can spend visiting cities in country X?

(A) 3
(B) 4
(C) 5
(D) 6
(E) 7

15. If Hannah spends three days in the cities of country Y and seven days in the cities of country Z, then which one of the following must be false?

(A) She visits more cities in country X than in country Y.
(B) She visits exactly two cities in country X.
(C) She visits more cities in country Z than in country X.
(D) She visits exactly two cities in country Z.
(E) She visits exactly three cities in country Z.

16. If the city of Nomo is in country X, and if Hannah spends as many days as possible in Nomo and as few days as possible in each of the other cities that she visits, then which one of the following must be true?

(A) Hannah cannot visit any other cities in country X.
(B) Hannah can visit four cities in country Y.
(C) Hannah can spend six days in Nomo.
(D) Hannah cannot spend more than four days in country Z.
(E) Hannah can visit, at most, a total of four cities in countries Y and Z.

17. If Hannah visits a combined total of four cities in countries X and Y, what is the greatest total number of days she can spend visiting cities in country Y?

(A) 6
(B) 7
(C) 8
(D) 9
(E) 10

J, K, L, M, N, and O are square ski chalets of the same size, which are positioned in two straight rows as shown below:

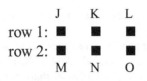

row 1: J K L
row 2: M N O

J is directly opposite M; K is directly opposite N; and L is directly opposite O. After a snowstorm, residents shovel a single continuous path that connects all of the chalets and meets the following conditions:

The path is composed of five straight segments, each of which directly connects exactly two of the chalets.
Each chalet is directly connected by a segment of the path to another chalet.
No chalet is directly connected by segments of the path to more than two other chalets.
No segment of the path crosses any other segment.
One segment of the path directly connects chalets J and N, and another segment directly connects chalets K and L.

18. Which one of the following statements could be true?

(A)   One segment of the path directly connects chalets M and K.
(B)   One segment of the path directly connects chalets M and L.
(C)   One segment of the path directly connects chalets M and O.
(D)   One segment of the path directly connects chalets J and K and another segment directly connects chalets K and M.
(E)   One segment of the path directly connects chalets O and L and another segment directly connects chalets O and N.

19. If one segment of the path directly connects chalets K and N, then the two chalets in which one of the following pairs must be directly connected to each other by a segment?

(A)   J and K
(B)   K and O
(C)   L and O
(D)   M and N
(E)   N and O

20. If a segment of the path directly connects chalets J and K, then the two chalets in which one of the following pairs must be directly connected to each other by a segment?

(A)   J and M
(B)   K and N
(C)   K and O
(D)   L and O
(E)   N and O

21. If one segment of the path directly connects chalets K and O, then which one of the following statements could be true?

(A)   Chalet J is directly connected to chalet M.
(B)   Chalet K is directly connected to chalet N.
(C)   Chalet L is directly connected to chalet O.
(D)   Chalet L is directly connected to exactly two chalets.
(E)   Chalet O is directly connected to exactly one chalet.

22. Which one of the following statements, if true, guarantees that one segment of the path directly connects chalets M and N?

(A)   One segment of the path directly connects chalets K and J.
(B)   One segment of the path directly connects chalets N and O.
(C)   One segment of the path directly connects chalet K and a chalet in row 2.
(D)   One segment of the path directly connects chalet L and a chalet in row 2.
(E)   One segment of the path directly connects chalet O and a chalet in row 1.

23. Which one of the following chalets cannot be directly connected by segments of the path to exactly two other chalets?

(A)   K
(B)   L
(C)   M
(D)   N
(E)   O

24. If no segment of the path directly connects any chalet in row 1 with the chalet in row 2 that is directly opposite it, then each of the following statements must be true EXCEPT:

(A)   A segment of the path directly connects chalets M and N.
(B)   A segment of the path directly connects chalets N and O.
(C)   Chalet L is directly connected to exactly one other chalet.
(D)   Chalet N is directly connected to exactly two other chalets.
(E)   Chalet O is directly connected to exactly two other chalets.

Petworld has exactly fourteen animals (three gerbils, three hamsters, three lizards, five snakes) that are kept in four separate cages (W, X, Y, Z) according to the following conditions:

Each cage contains exactly two, four, or six animals.

Any cage containing a gerbil also contains at least one hamster; any cage containing a hamster also contains at least one gerbil.

Any cage containing a lizard also contains at least one snake; any cage containing a snake also contains at least one lizard.

Neither cage Y nor cage Z contains a gerbil.

Neither cage W nor cage X contains a lizard.

1. Which one of the following could be a complete and accurate list of the animals kept in cages W and Y?

   (A) W: one gerbil and one hamster
        Y: two lizards and two snakes
   (B) W: one gerbil and two hamsters
        Y: one lizard and three snakes
   (C) W: two gerbils and two hamsters
        Y: one lizard and four snakes
   (D) W: two gerbils and two hamsters
        Y: three lizards and one snake
   (E) W: two gerbils and two lizards
        Y: two hamsters and two snakes

2. If there are exactly two hamsters in cage W and the number of gerbils in cage X is equal to the number of snakes in cage Y, then the number of snakes in cage Z must be exactly

   (A) one
   (B) two
   (C) three
   (D) four
   (E) five

3. If cage Z contains exactly twice as many lizards as cage Y, which one of the following can be true?

   (A) Cage Y contains exactly two lizards.
   (B) Cage Y contains exactly two snakes.
   (C) Cage Y contains exactly four animals.
   (D) Cage Z contains exactly three snakes.
   (E) Cage Z contains exactly two animals.

4. If the number of animals in cage W is equal to the number of animals in cage Z, then which one of the following can be true?

   (A) Cage W contains exactly six animals.
   (B) Cage X contains exactly six animals.
   (C) Cage Y contains exactly one snake.
   (D) Cage Y contains exactly three snakes.
   (E) Cage Z contains exactly four snakes.

5. If cage Y contains six animals, which one of the following must be true?

   (A) Cage W contains two gerbils.
   (B) Cage X contains four animals.
   (C) Cage Z contains two snakes.
   (D) The number of snakes in cage Y is equal to the number of lizards in cage Y.
   (E) The number of snakes in cage Z is equal to the number of lizards in cage Z.

6. At most, how many snakes can occupy cage Y at any one time?

   (A) one
   (B) two
   (C) three
   (D) four
   (E) five

Each of seven judges voted for or else against granting Datalog Corporation's petition. Each judge is categorized as conservative, moderate, or liberal, and no judge is assigned more than one of those labels. Two judges are conservatives, two are moderates, and three are liberals. The following is known about how the judges voted:

> If the two conservatives and at least one liberal voted the same way as each other, then both moderates voted that way.
> If the three liberals voted the same way as each other, then no conservative voted that way.
> At least two of the judges voted for Datalog, and at least two voted against Datalog.
> At least one conservative voted against Datalog.

13. If the two moderates did not vote the same way as each other, then which one of the following could be true?

    (A)   No conservative and exactly two liberals voted for Datalog.
    (B)   Exactly one conservative and exactly one liberal voted for Datalog.
    (C)   Exactly one conservative and all three liberals voted for Datalog.
    (D)   Exactly two conservatives and exactly one liberal voted for Datalog.
    (E)   Exactly two conservatives and exactly two liberals voted for Datalog.

14. Which one of the following must be true?

    (A)   At least one conservative voted for Datalog.
    (B)   At least one liberal voted against Datalog.
    (C)   At least one liberal voted for Datalog.
    (D)   At least one moderate voted against Datalog.
    (E)   At least one moderate voted for Datalog.

15. If the three liberals all voted the same way as each other, which one of the following must be true?

    (A)   Both moderates voted for Datalog.
    (B)   Both moderates voted against Datalog.
    (C)   One conservative voted for Datalog and one conservative voted against Datalog.
    (D)   One moderate voted for Datalog and one moderate voted against Datalog.
    (E)   All three liberals voted for Datalog.

16. If exactly two judges voted against Datalog, then which one of the following must be true?

    (A)   Both moderates voted for Datalog.
    (B)   Exactly one conservative voted for Datalog.
    (C)   No conservative voted for Datalog.
    (D)   Exactly two liberals voted for Datalog.
    (E)   Exactly three liberals voted for Datalog.

17. Each of the following could be a complete and accurate list of those judges who voted for Datalog EXCEPT

    (A)   two liberals
    (B)   one conservative, one liberal
    (C)   two moderates, three liberals
    (D)   one conservative, two moderates, two liberals
    (E)   one conservative, two moderates, three liberals

18. If the two conservatives voted the same way as each other, but the liberals did not all vote the same way as each other, then each of the following must be true EXCEPT:

    (A)   Both conservatives voted against Datalog.
    (B)   Both moderates voted for Datalog.
    (C)   At least one liberal voted against Datalog.
    (D)   Exactly two liberals voted for Datalog.
    (E)   Exactly five of the judges voted against Datalog.

An official is assigning five runners—Larry, Ned, Olivia, Patricia, and Sonja—to parallel lanes numbered consecutively 1 through 5. The official will also assign each runner to represent a different charity—F, G, H, J, and K—not necessarily in order of the runner's names as given. The following ordering restrictions apply:

The runner representing K is assigned to lane 4.

Patricia is assigned to the only lane between the lanes of the runners representing F and G.

There are exactly two lanes between Olivia's lane and the lane of the runner representing G.

Sonja is assigned to a higher-numbered lane than the lane to which Ned is assigned.

19. Which one of the following is a possible assignment of runners to lanes by the charity they represent?

	1	2	3	4	5
(A)	F	G	H	K	J
(B)	G	H	J	K	F
(C)	G	K	F	J	H
(D)	H	J	G	K	F
(E)	J	H	F	K	G

20. The lane to which Patricia is assigned must be a lane that is

(A) next to the lane to which Larry is assigned
(B) next to the lane to which Ned is assigned
(C) separated by exactly one lane from the lane to which Ned is assigned
(D) separated by exactly one lane from the lane to which Olivia is assigned
(E) separated by exactly one lane from the lane to which Sonja is assigned

21. If Olivia is assigned to lane 2, which one of the following assignments must be made?

	Charity	Lane
(A)	F	1
(B)	G	5
(C)	H	1
(D)	H	3
(E)	J	5

22. Which one of the following is a complete and accurate list of runners each of whom could be the runner representing F?

(A) Larry, Ned
(B) Patricia, Sonja
(C) Larry, Ned, Olivia
(D) Larry, Ned, Sonja
(E) Ned, Patricia, Sonja

23. If Ned is the runner representing J, then it must be true that

(A) the runner representing G is assigned to lane 1
(B) the runner representing H is assigned to lane 2
(C) Larry is the runner representing K
(D) Olivia is the runner representing F
(E) Patricia is the runner representing H

24. If Larry represents J, which one of the following could be the assignment of runners to lanes?

	1	2	3	4	5
(A)	Larry	Olivia	Ned	Patricia	Sonja
(B)	Larry	Ned	Olivia	Sonja	Patricia
(C)	Larry	Sonja	Patricia	Ned	Olivia
(D)	Ned	Olivia	Larry	Patricia	Sonja
(E)	Ned	Sonja	Olivia	Patricia	Larry

A square parking lot has exactly eight lights—numbered 1 through 8—situated along its perimeter as diagramed below.

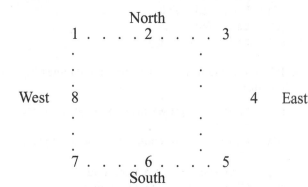

North

1 . . . . 2 3

West   8   4   East

7 . . . . 6 5

South

The lot must always be illuminated in such a way that the following specifications are met:

At least one of any three consecutively numbered lights is off.

Light 8 is on.

Neither light 2 nor light 7 is on when light 1 is on.

At least one of the three lights on each side is on.

If any side has exactly one of its three lights on, then that light is its center light.

Two of the lights on the north side are on.

6. Which one of the following could be a complete and accurate list of lights that are on together?

(A)   1, 3, 5, 7
(B)   2, 4, 6, 8
(C)   2, 3, 5, 6, 8
(D)   3, 4, 6, 7, 8
(E)   1, 2, 4, 5, 6, 8

7. Which one of the following lights must be on?

(A)   light 2
(B)   light 3
(C)   light 4
(D)   light 5
(E)   light 6

8. If light 1 is off, which one of the following is a light that must also be off?

(A)   light 3
(B)   light 4
(C)   light 5
(D)   light 6
(E)   light 7

9. Which one of the following statements must be true?

(A)   If light 2 is on, then light 6 is off.
(B)   If light 3 is on, then light 2 is on.
(C)   If light 4 is on, then light 3 is off.
(D)   If light 5 is off, then light 4 is on.
(E)   If light 6 is off, then light 1 is on.

10. If light 5 is on, which one of the following could be true?

(A)   Light 1 is off and light 6 is off.
(B)   Light 1 is on and light 7 is on.
(C)   Light 2 is off and light 4 is on.
(D)   Light 2 is off and light 6 is off.
(E)   Light 6 is on and light 7 is on.

11. If light 4 is on, each of the following statements must be true EXCEPT:

(A)   Light 1 is on.
(B)   Light 2 is on.
(C)   Light 5 is off.
(D)   Light 6 is on.
(E)   Light 7 is off.

12. Suppose that it is no longer part of the specifications that two lights on the north side be on. If all of the other original specifications remain the same, and if exactly one light on the north side is on, which one of the following statements could be false?

(A)   Light 1 is off.
(B)   Light 2 is on.
(C)   Light 3 is off.
(D)   Light 4 is on.
(E)   Light 5 is on.

A florist is making three corsages from four types of flowers: gardenias, orchids, roses, and violets. Each of the corsages will contain exactly three flowers. The nine flowers used in the corsages must include at least one flower from each of the four types, and at least twice as many roses as orchids must be used. The corsages must also meet the following specifications:

Corsage 1 must contain exactly two types of flowers.
Corsage 2 must contain at least one rose.
Corsage 3 must contain at least one gardenia but no orchids.

1. Which one of the following is an acceptable selection of flowers for the three corsages?

	Corsage 1	Corsage 2	Corsage 3
(A)	2 gardenias 1 rose	1 orchid 1 rose 1 violet	1 gardenia 1 orchid 1 violet
(B)	2 orchids 1 rose	2 orchids 1 rose	2 gardenias 1 rose
(C)	2 orchids 1 rose	3 roses	1 gardenia 2 violets
(D)	1 gardenia 1 orchid 1 rose	1 gardenia 1 rose 1 violet	1 gardenia 1 rose 1 violet
(E)	1 orchid 2 roses	3 violets	3 gardenias

2. The maximum total number of roses that can be used in the three corsages is

(A) three
(B) four
(C) five
(D) six
(E) seven

3. If corsage 1 contains two orchids and one rose, what is the maximum total number of violets that the florist can use in making the three corsages?

(A) one
(B) two
(C) three
(D) four
(E) five

4. If corsage 2 is exactly the same as corsage 3, the nine flowers used in the corsages can include exactly

(A) two orchids
(B) three gardenias
(C) three roses
(D) five roses
(E) five violets

5. If two of the corsages contain at least one orchid each, then the flowers in corsage 2 must include at least

(A) one gardenia and one orchid
(B) one gardenia and one rose
(C) one orchid and one rose
(D) one orchid and one violet
(E) one rose and one violet

6. If the greatest possible number of violets is used in the three corsages, the florist must use

(A) exactly one rose and exactly one gardenia
(B) exactly one orchid and exactly four violets
(C) exactly two orchids
(D) exactly two roses
(E) exactly six violets

7. If corsage 1 contains at least one gardenia and at least one violet, and if corsage 3 contains three different types of flowers, which one of the following could be used to make corsage 2?

(A) one rose, one orchid, and one gardenia
(B) one rose and two orchids
(C) one rose and two violets
(D) two roses and one gardenia
(E) two roses and one violet

Six reviewers—Frank, George, Hilda, Jackie, Karl, and Lena—will review four movies—*Mystery, Retreat, Seasonings,* and *Wolves*—according to the following conditions:

Each reviewer reviews exactly one movie, and each movie is reviewed by at least one of the six reviewers.
Hilda reviews the same movie as Frank.
Lena reviews the same movie as exactly one other reviewer.
George reviews *Mystery.*
Jackie reviews either *Mystery* or else *Wolves.*
Hilda does not review *Wolves.*

6. If Lena reviews *Seasonings,* which one of the following must be true?

(A) Hilda reviews *Retreat.*
(B) Jackie reviews *Seasonings.*
(C) Karl reviews *Mystery.*
(D) Karl reviews *Retreat.*
(E) Karl reviews *Wolves.*

7. If Karl does not review *Seasonings,* which one of the following must be true?

(A) Lena reviews *Mystery.*
(B) Lena reviews *Retreat.*
(C) Lena reviews *Seasonings.*
(D) Frank and Hilda review *Retreat.*
(E) Frank and Hilda review *Seasonings.*

8. Which one of the following is a complete and accurate list of the movies each of which could be the movie that Lena reviews?

(A) *Mystery, Retreat*
(B) *Retreat, Seasonings*
(C) *Mystery, Seasonings, Wolves*
(D) *Retreat, Seasonings, Wolves*
(E) *Mystery, Retreat, Seasonings, Wolves*

9. Which one of the following can be true?

(A) Frank and George review *Mystery.*
(B) Frank and Lena review *Wolves.*
(C) George and Jackie review *Mystery.*
(D) Karl reviews *Wolves* and Lena reviews *Mystery.*
(E) Lena reviews *Retreat* and Frank reviews *Seasonings.*

10. Lena can review any of the following EXCEPT

(A) *Mystery* with George
(B) *Mystery* with Karl
(C) *Retreat* with Karl
(D) *Seasonings* with Karl
(E) *Wolves* with Jackie

11. If Karl reviews the same movie as exactly one other reviewer, which one of the following is a complete and accurate list of the movies any one of which could be the movie that these two reviewers review?

(A) *Mystery, Retreat*
(B) *Mystery, Seasonings*
(C) *Retreat, Seasonings*
(D) *Mystery, Seasonings, Wolves*
(E) *Retreat, Seasonings, Wolves*

12. Which one of the following is an acceptable assignment of reviewers to movies?

	Mystery	*Retreat*	*Seasonings*	*Wolves*
(A)	George	Frank, Hilda	Jackie, Lena	Karl
(B)	George	Frank, Hilda	Karl, Lena	Jackie
(C)	George	Karl, Lena	Jackie	Frank, Hilda
(D)	George, Karl	Frank, Hilda	Lena	Jackie
(E)	Jackie	George, Lena	Frank, Hilda	Karl

A fire chief is determining the work schedules of five firefighters: Fuentes, Graber, Howell, Iman, and Jackson. The schedule must meet the following conditions:

Except for Saturday and Sunday, when none of them works, exactly one of the firefighters works each day.

None of the firefighters can work more than two days per week.

No firefighter works on two consecutive days.

Fuentes never works later in the week than Jackson.

If Howell works, then Graber must work on the following day.

7. Which one of the following CANNOT be a Monday-to-Friday work schedule?

(A) Fuentes, Iman, Fuentes, Jackson, Iman
(B) Fuentes, Jackson, Howell, Graber, Fuentes
(C) Graber, Fuentes, Graber, Fuentes, Jackson
(D) Graber, Howell, Graber, Fuentes, Jackson
(E) Howell, Graber, Iman, Graber, Iman

8. If each firefighter is required to have at least two consecutive days off during the Monday-to-Friday workweek, which one of the following could be a possible work schedule?

(A) Howell, Graber, Howell, Graber, Iman
(B) Howell, Howell, Graber, Fuentes, Iman
(C) Iman, Fuentes, Jackson, Iman, Iman
(D) Fuentes, Howell, Graber, Fuentes, Jackson
(E) Jackson, Howell, Graber, Iman, Fuentes

9. If both Fuentes and Jackson work during a week, which one of the following statements CANNOT be true?

(A) Fuentes works on Monday and Wednesday.
(B) Jackson works on Monday and Wednesday.
(C) Fuentes works on Tuesday and Thursday.
(D) Jackson works on Tuesday and Thursday.
(E) Jackson works on Wednesday and Friday.

10. If Fuentes works two days during the week and Jackson works on Thursday, which one of the following statements could be true?

(A) Fuentes works on Tuesday.
(B) Graber works on Tuesday.
(C) Howell works on Tuesday.
(D) Graber works on Wednesday.
(E) Howell works on Wednesday.

11. If Graber does not work during the week, which one of the following statements must be true?

(A) Fuentes works exactly one day during the week.
(B) Fuentes works exactly two days during the week.
(C) Iman works exactly one day during the week.
(D) Iman works exactly two days during the week.
(E) Jackson works exactly one day during the week.

Four apprentices—Louis, Madelyn, Nora, and Oliver—are initially assigned to projects Q, R, S, and T, respectively. During the year in which they are apprentices, two reassignments of apprentices to projects will be made, each time according to a different one of the following plans, which can be used in any order:

Plan 1. The apprentice assigned to project Q switches projects with the apprentice assigned to project S and the apprentice assigned to project R switches projects with the apprentice assigned to project T.

Plan 2. The apprentice assigned to project S switches projects with the apprentice assigned to project T.

Plan 3. Louis and Madelyn switch projects with each other.

20. Which one of the following must be true after the second reassignment of apprentices to projects during the year if that reassignment assigns Nora to project T?

(A) Louis is assigned to project S.
(B) Madelyn is assigned to project R.
(C) Madelyn is assigned to project S.
(D) Oliver is assigned to project R.
(E) Oliver is assigned to project S.

21. Which one of the following could be true after only one reassignment during the year?

(A) Louis is assigned to project T.
(B) Nora is assigned to project R.
(C) Oliver is assigned to project Q.
(D) Louis and Nora each remain assigned to the same projects as before.
(E) Nora and Oliver each remain assigned to the same projects as before.

22. If at some time during the year, Louis is reassigned to project R, which one of the following could have been the assignment of apprentices to the projects immediately before the reassignment?

(A) Q: Louis; R: Madelyn; S: Oliver; T: Nora
(B) Q: Louis; R: Nora; S: Oliver; T: Madelyn
(C) Q: Nora; R: Madelyn; S: Louis; T: Oliver
(D) Q: Nora; R: Oliver; S: Louis; T: Madelyn
(E) Q: Oliver; R: Nora; S: Louis; T: Madelyn

23. Which one of the following is an acceptable assignment of apprentices to the projects after only one reassignment during the year?

(A) Q: Louis; R: Madelyn; S: Nora; T: Oliver
(B) Q: Madelyn; R: Louis; S: Nora; T: Oliver
(C) Q: Madelyn; R: Oliver; S: Nora; T: Louis
(D) Q: Nora; R: Louis; S: Oliver; T: Madelyn
(E) Q: Nora; R: Madelyn; S: Oliver; T: Louis

24. If the first reassignment is made according to plan 1, which one of the following must be true?

(A) Louis is assigned to project T as a result of the second reassignment.
(B) Madelyn is assigned to project Q as a result of the second reassignment.
(C) Madelyn is assigned to project T as a result of the second reassignment.
(D) Oliver is assigned to project S as a result of the second reassignment.
(E) Oliver is assigned to project T as a result of the second reassignment.

A piano instructor will schedule exactly one lesson for each of six students—Grace, Henry, Janet, Steve, Tom, and Una—one lesson per day for six consecutive days. The schedule must conform to the following conditions:

Henry's lesson is later in the schedule than Janet's lesson.

Una's lesson is later in the schedule than Steve's lesson.

Steve's lesson is exactly three days after Grace's lesson.

Janet's lesson is on the first day or else the third day.

1. If Janet's lesson is scheduled for the first day, then the lesson for which one of the following students must be scheduled for the sixth day?

   (A) Grace
   (B) Henry
   (C) Steve
   (D) Tom
   (E) Una

2. For which one of the following students is there an acceptable schedule in which the student's lesson is on the third day and another acceptable schedule in which the student's lesson is on the fifth day? ·

   (A) Grace
   (B) Henry
   (C) Steve
   (D) Tom
   (E) Una

3. Which one of the following is a complete and accurate list of the students any one of whom could be the student whose lesson is scheduled for the second day?

   (A) Grace
   (B) Tom
   (C) Grace, Tom
   (D) Henry, Tom
   (E) Grace, Henry, Tom

4. If Henry's lesson is scheduled for a day either immediately before or immediately after Tom's lesson, then Grace's lesson must be scheduled for the

   (A) first day
   (B) second day
   (C) third day
   (D) fourth day
   (E) fifth day

5. If Janet's lesson is scheduled for the third day, which one of the following could be true?

   (A) Grace's lesson is scheduled for a later day than Henry's lesson.
   (B) Grace's lesson is scheduled for a later day than Una's lesson.
   (C) Henry's lesson is scheduled for a later day than Una's lesson.
   (D) Tom's lesson is scheduled for a later day than Henry's lesson.
   (E) Tom's lesson is scheduled for a later day than Una's lesson.

6. Which one of the following is a complete and accurate list of days any one of which could be the day for which Tom's lesson is scheduled?

   (A) first, second, third
   (B) second, third, fourth
   (C) second, fifth, sixth
   (D) first, second, third, fourth
   (E) second, third, fourth, sixth

A science student has exactly four flasks—1, 2, 3, and 4—originally containing a red, a blue, a green, and an orange chemical, respectively. An experiment consists of mixing exactly two of these chemicals together by completely emptying the contents of one of the flasks into another of the flasks. The following conditions apply:

The product of an experiment cannot be used in further experiments.

Mixing the contents of 1 and 2 produces a red chemical.

Mixing the contents of 2 and 3 produces an orange chemical.

Mixing the contents of 3 with the contents of either 1 or 4 produces a blue chemical.

Mixing the contents of 4 with the contents of either 1 or 2 produces a green chemical.

18. If the student performs exactly one experiment, which one of the following could be the colors of the chemicals in the resulting three nonempty flasks?

   (A)   blue, blue, green
   (B)   blue, orange, orange
   (C)   blue, orange, red
   (D)   green, green, red
   (E)   green, orange, orange

19. If the student performs exactly two experiments, which one of the following could be the colors of the chemicals in the resulting two nonempty flasks?

   (A)   blue, blue
   (B)   blue, orange
   (C)   blue, red
   (D)   green, red
   (E)   orange, orange

20. If the student performs exactly one experiment and none of the resulting three nonempty flasks contains a red chemical, which one of the following could be the colors of the chemicals in the three flasks?

   (A)   blue, blue, green
   (B)   blue, green, green
   (C)   blue, green, orange
   (D)   blue, orange, orange
   (E)   green, green, orange

21. If the student performs exactly one experiment and exactly one of the resulting three nonempty flasks contains a blue chemical, which one of the following must be the colors of the chemicals in the other two flasks?

   (A)   both green
   (B)   both orange
   (C)   both red
   (D)   one green and one red
   (E)   one orange and one red

22. If the student will perform exactly two experiments and after the first experiment exactly one of the resulting three nonempty flasks contains an orange chemical, then in the second experiment the student could mix together the contents of flasks

   (A)   1 and 2
   (B)   1 and 3
   (C)   1 and 4
   (D)   2 and 3
   (E)   3 and 4

23. If the student performs exactly one experiment and none of the resulting three nonempty flasks contains an orange chemical, then the student must have mixed the contents of

   (A)   flask 1 with flask 2
   (B)   flask 1 with flask 4
   (C)   flask 2 with flask 4
   (D)   flask 2 with one of the other flasks
   (E)   flask 4 with one of the other flasks

24. If the student performs exactly two experiments and exactly one of the resulting two nonempty flasks contains an orange chemical, then it must be true that the contents of the other nonempty flask is

   (A)   obtained by mixing flasks 1 and 2
   (B)   obtained by mixing flasks 2 and 4
   (C)   blue
   (D)   green
   (E)   red

Ron washed a total of seven objects after eating his lunch. Two of the objects were pieces of china: a mug and a plate. Two were pieces of glassware: a water glass and a juice glass. Three were utensils: a fork, a knife, and a spoon. Ron washed the two pieces of china consecutively, the two glasses consecutively, and the three utensils consecutively. He washed the objects as follows:

Ron washed each of the objects exactly once.
Ron washed the glassware after either the china or the utensils but not after both.
He washed the knife before the spoon, and he washed the mug before the plate.
He did not wash any two objects at the same time.

7. Which one of the following statements CANNOT be true?

   (A) Ron washed the fork first.
   (B) Ron washed the fork second.
   (C) Ron washed the mug first.
   (D) Ron washed the plate second.
   (E) Ron washed the plate third.

8. Which one of the following statements can be true?

   (A) Ron washed the knife second.
   (B) Ron washed the knife seventh.
   (C) Ron washed the mug second.
   (D) Ron washed the mug third.
   (E) Ron washed the mug fourth.

9. Which one of the following CANNOT be an accurate list of the objects Ron washed second, third, and fourth, respectively?

   (A) fork, spoon, water glass
   (B) knife, fork, juice glass
   (C) knife, spoon, juice glass
   (D) knife, spoon, water glass
   (E) plate, water glass, juice glass

10. It is NOT possible that Ron washed the knife

    (A) first
    (B) second
    (C) third
    (D) fifth
    (E) sixth

11. If Ron washed the spoon immediately before the fork, then which one of the following statements can be true?

    (A) He washed the knife second.
    (B) He washed the knife third.
    (C) He washed the plate third.
    (D) He washed the plate sixth.
    (E) He washed the plate seventh.

12. If Ron washed a glass and the knife consecutively, but not necessarily in that order, then which one of the following statements must be false?

    (A) He washed the fork before the plate.
    (B) He washed the fork before the spoon.
    (C) He washed the juice glass before the knife.
    (D) He washed the plate before the water glass.
    (E) He washed the spoon before the fork.

Four people—Fritz, Gina, Helen, and Jerry—have formed a car pool to commute to work together six days a week from Monday through Saturday. Each day exactly one of the people drives. The schedule of the car pool's drivers for any given week must meet the following conditions:

Each person drives on at least one day.

No person drives on two consecutive days.

Fritz does not drive on Monday.

Jerry drives on Wednesday or Saturday or both, and he may also drive on other days.

If Gina drives on Monday, then Jerry does not drive on Saturday.

14. Which one of the following could be the schedule of drivers for one week, for the days Monday through Saturday, respectively?

(A)   Gina, Fritz, Jerry, Helen, Gina, Gina
(B)   Gina, Fritz, Jerry, Helen, Fritz, Jerry
(C)   Helen, Fritz, Gina, Jerry, Helen, Fritz
(D)   Helen, Gina, Jerry, Fritz, Helen, Fritz
(E)   Helen, Gina, Jerry, Helen, Jerry, Gina

15. Which one of the following could be true of one week's schedule of drivers?

(A)   Fritz drives on both Wednesday and Saturday.
(B)   Gina drives on both Monday and Wednesday.
(C)   Jerry drives on both Tuesday and Friday.
(D)   Gina drives on Monday and Jerry drives on Thursday.
(E)   Jerry drives on Wednesday and Gina drives on Saturday.

16. If during one week Jerry drives on Wednesday and Saturday only, which one of the following must be true of that week?

(A)   Fritz drives on Tuesday.
(B)   Gina drives on Friday.
(C)   Helen drives on Monday.
(D)   Fritz drives on exactly two days.
(E)   Helen drives on exactly two days.

17. If during one week Gina drives on Monday and Saturday only, which one of the following must be true of that week?

(A)   One other person besides Gina drives on exactly two days.
(B)   The person who drives on Wednesday does not drive on Friday.
(C)   Helen drives on a day immediately before a day on which Fritz drives.
(D)   Either Fritz or Helen drives on Friday.
(E)   Either Helen or Jerry drives on Tuesday.

18. Which one of the following CANNOT be true of one week's schedule of drivers?

(A)   Fritz drives on Tuesday and Gina drives on Friday.
(B)   Gina drives on Monday and Jerry drives on Tuesday.
(C)   Gina drives on Monday and Jerry drives on Friday.
(D)   Helen drives on Monday and Jerry drives on Tuesday.
(E)   Helen drives on Tuesday and Jerry drives on Friday.

19. If during one week Fritz drives exactly twice but he drives on neither Tuesday nor Wednesday, which one of the following could be true of that week?

(A)   One person drives exactly three times during the week.
(B)   Three people drive exactly one time each during the week.
(C)   Jerry drives on no day that is immediately before a day on which Fritz drives.
(D)   Gina drives on Wednesday.
(E)   Jerry drives on Friday.

Game #15: September 1995 Questions 7-12

Four lions—F, G, H, J—and two tigers—K and M—will be assigned to exactly six stalls, one animal per stall. The stalls are arranged as follows:

First Row: 1 2 3

Second Row: 4 5 6

The only stalls that face each other are stalls 1 and 4, stalls 2 and 5, and stalls 3 and 6. The following conditions apply:

The tigers' stalls cannot face each other.
A lion must be assigned to stall 1.
H must be assigned to stall 6.
J must be assigned to a stall numbered one higher than K's stall.
K cannot be assigned to the stall that faces H's stall.

7. Which one of the following must be true?

(A) F is assigned to an even-numbered stall.
(B) F is assigned to stall 1.
(C) J is assigned to stall 2 or else stall 3.
(D) J is assigned to stall 3 or else stall 4.
(E) K is assigned to stall 2 or else stall 4.

8. Which one of the following could be true?

(A) F's stall is numbered one higher than J's stall.
(B) H's stall faces M's stall.
(C) J is assigned to stall 4.
(D) K's stall faces J's stall.
(E) K's stall is in a different row than J's stall.

9. Which one of the following must be true?

(A) A tiger is assigned to stall 2.
(B) A tiger is assigned to stall 5.
(C) K's stall is in a different row from M's stall.
(D) Each tiger is assigned to an even-numbered stall.
(E) Each lion is assigned to a stall that faces a tiger's stall.

10. If K's stall is in the same row as H's stall, which one of the following must be true?

(A) F's stall is in the same row as J's stall.
(B) F is assigned to a lower-numbered stall than G.
(C) G is assigned to a lower-numbered stall than M.
(D) G's stall faces H's stall.
(E) M's stall is in the same row as G's stall.

11. If J is assigned to stall 3, which one of the following could be true?

(A) F is assigned to stall 2.
(B) F is assigned to stall 4.
(C) G is assigned to stall 1.
(D) G is assigned to stall 4.
(E) M is assigned to stall 5.

12. Which one of the following must be true?

(A) A tiger is assigned to stall 2.
(B) A tiger is assigned to stall 4.
(C) A tiger is assigned to stall 5.
(D) A lion is assigned to stall 3.
(E) A lion is assigned to stall 4.

Eight people—Jack, Karen, Laura, Mark, Nick, Owen, Peggy, and Ruth—will be placed on two four-person teams—X and Y—for a relay race that is run in four successive legs: first, second, third, and fourth. The teams race concurrently. Each team member runs exactly one of the legs, one team member per leg, according to the following conditions:

> Jack is on the same team as Karen.
> Karen is not on the same team as Nick.
> Ruth runs an earlier leg of the race than Peggy runs, whether or not they are on the same team as each other.
> Mark and Nick are both on team Y.
> Neither Jack nor Mark runs third.
> Karen and Laura both run second.
> Owen runs fourth.

18. Which one of the following must be true?

    (A) If Jack and Owen are assigned to the same team as each other, Jack runs first.
    (B) If Jack and Peggy are assigned to the same team as each other, Jack runs fourth.
    (C) If Jack and Ruth are assigned to the same team as each other, Ruth runs third.
    (D) If Mark and Owen are assigned to the same team as each other, Mark runs fourth.
    (E) If Mark and Ruth are assigned to the same team as each other, Ruth runs third.

19. If Ruth is assigned to team X, which one of the following is a complete and accurate list of the legs that she could run?

    (A) first
    (B) second
    (C) first, second
    (D) first, third
    (E) second, third

20. If Owen and Ruth are assigned to the same team as each other, which one of the following must be true?

    (A) Mark runs fourth.
    (B) Nick runs first.
    (C) Nick runs fourth.
    (D) Peggy runs first.
    (E) Peggy runs fourth.

21. Any of the following can be true EXCEPT:

    (A) Jack runs first.
    (B) Mark runs fourth.
    (C) Nick runs first.
    (D) Nick and Peggy both run third.
    (E) Owen and Peggy both run fourth.

22. If Ruth and Peggy are assigned to the same team as each other, which one of the following must be true?

    (A) Jack runs first.
    (B) Mark runs fourth.
    (C) Nick runs third.
    (D) Peggy runs third.
    (E) Ruth runs first.

23. Any of the following can be true EXCEPT:

    (A) Jack runs fourth.
    (B) Nick runs fourth.
    (C) Peggy runs fourth.
    (D) Ruth runs first.
    (E) Ruth runs third.

24. If Peggy runs third on the same team to which Jack is assigned, which one of the following must be true?

    (A) Jack runs the first leg on the team to which he is assigned.
    (B) Ruth runs the first leg on the team to which she is assigned.
    (C) Owen runs on the same team as Jack.
    (D) Owen runs on the same team as Mark.
    (E) Ruth runs on the same team as Mark.

A college offers one course in each of three subjects—mathematics, nutrition, and oceanography—in the fall and again in the spring. Students' book orders for these course offerings are kept in six folders, numbered 1 through 6, from which labels identifying the folders' contents are missing. The following is known:

Each folder contains only the orders for one of the six course offerings.

Folder 1 contains orders for the same subject as folder 2 does.

The orders in folder 3 are for a different subject than are the orders in folder 4.

The fall mathematics orders are in folder 1 or else folder 4.

The spring oceanography orders are in folder 1 or else folder 4.

The spring nutrition orders are not in folder 5.

7. Which one of the following could be the list of the contents of the folders, in order from folder 1 to folder 6?

(A) fall mathematics, spring mathematics, fall oceanography, fall nutrition, spring nutrition, spring oceanography

(B) fall oceanography, spring nutrition, fall nutrition, fall mathematics, spring mathematics, spring oceanography

(C) spring mathematics, fall mathematics, spring nutrition, fall oceanography, fall nutrition, spring oceanography

(D) spring oceanography, fall oceanography, fall nutrition, fall mathematics, spring mathematics, spring nutrition

(E) spring oceanography, fall oceanography, spring mathematics, fall mathematics, fall nutrition, spring nutrition

8. Which one of the following statements must be false?

(A) The spring mathematics orders are in folder 3.

(B) The fall nutrition orders are in folder 3.

(C) The spring oceanography orders are in folder 1.

(D) The spring nutrition orders are in folder 6.

(E) The fall oceanography orders are in folder 5.

9. If the fall oceanography orders are in folder 2, then which one of the following statements could be true?

(A) The spring mathematics orders are in folder 4.

(B) The spring mathematics orders are in folder 6.

(C) The fall nutrition orders are in folder 1.

(D) The spring nutrition orders are in neither folder 3 nor folder 6.

(E) Neither the spring nor the fall nutrition orders are in folder 3.

10. Which one of the following statements could be true?

(A) The spring mathematics orders are in folder 1.

(B) The fall oceanography orders are in folder 1.

(C) The fall nutrition orders are in folder 4, and the fall oceanography orders are in folder 6.

(D) The fall oceanography orders are in folder 2, and the spring oceanography orders are in folder 1.

(E) The spring oceanography orders are in folder 1, and neither the spring nor the fall nutrition orders are in folder 3.

11. If the fall oceanography orders are in folder 2, then for exactly how many of the remaining five folders can it be deduced which course offering's orders are in that folder?

(A) one

(B) two

(C) three

(D) four

(E) five

12. Which one of the following lists a pair of folders that must together contain orders for two different subjects?

(A) 3 and 5

(B) 4 and 5

(C) 3 and 6

(D) 4 and 6

(E) 5 and 6

13. Which one of the following could be true?

(A) The fall mathematics and spring oceanography orders are in folders with consecutive numbers.

(B) Folder 5 contains the orders for a spring course in a subject other than mathematics.

(C) Folder 6 contains the orders for a subject other than nutrition.

(D) The mathematics orders are in folders 1 and 4.

(E) The orders for the fall courses are in folders 1, 3, and 6.

In a theater company, four two-day workshops—Lighting, Production, Rehearsals, and Staging—are conducted over the course of five days, Monday through Friday. The workshops are conducted in a manner consistent with the following constraints:

The two days on which a given workshop is in session are consecutive.

On each of the five days, at least one, but no more than two, of the workshops are in session.

The workshops on Production and Rehearsals begin no earlier than the day immediately following the second day of the workshop on Lighting.

8. Which one of the following could be true?

(A) Only one workshop is in session on Thursday.
(B) Only one workshop is in session on Friday.
(C) The workshop on Rehearsals is in session on Tuesday.
(D) The workshop on Staging is in session on Thursday.
(E) The workshops in Rehearsals and Production are both in session on Wednesday.

9. Which one of the following could be true?

(A) The workshop on Lighting is in session on Wednesday, and the workshop on Rehearsals is in session on Tuesday.
(B) The workshop on Lighting is in session on Wednesday, and the only workshop in session on Thursday is the workshop on Rehearsals.
(C) The workshop on Lighting is in session on Wednesday, and the only workshop in session on Monday is the workshop on Staging.
(D) The workshop on Lighting is in session on Monday, and the only workshop in session on Thursday is the workshop on Staging.
(E) The workshops on Lighting and Production are both in session on Wednesday.

10. If the workshop on Production is in session on Wednesday, which one of the following must be true?

(A) The workshop on Lighting is in session on Monday.
(B) The workshop on Rehearsals is in session on Wednesday.
(C) The workshop on Staging is in session on Thursday.
(D) The workshop on Staging is in session on Monday.
(E) The workshop on Staging is in session on Wednesday.

11. If the workshop on Production is the only workshop in session on Friday, which one of the following must be false?

(A) The workshop on Lighting is in session both on Tuesday and on Wednesday.
(B) The workshop on Rehearsals is in session both on Wednesday and on Thursday.
(C) The workshop on Staging is in session both on Monday and on Tuesday.
(D) The workshop on Lighting is in session on the same two days as is the workshop on Staging.
(E) The workshop on Rehearsals is in session on a day when the workshop on Staging is also in session.

12. If the workshop on Lighting is the only workshop in session on Monday, which one of the following could be true?

(A) The workshops on Rehearsals and Staging are both in session on Tuesday.
(B) The workshop on Rehearsals is the only workshop in session on Wednesday.
(C) The workshop on Staging is the only workshop in session on Wednesday.
(D) The workshops on Staging and Rehearsals are both in session on Wednesday and on Thursday.
(E) The workshops on Staging and Production are both in session on Thursday.

ANSWER KEY

Chapter Two: Basic Linear Games

Game #1: October 1991 Questions 6-12   *6. D 7. E 8. A 9. E 10. C 11. B 12. C*

Game #2: December 1991 Questions 8-13   *8. C 9. A 10. C 11. A 12. A 13. D*

Game #3: June 1992 Questions 1-6   *1. C 2. D 3. E 4. E 5. C 6. E*

Game #4: February 1993 Questions 1-7   *1. C 2. A 3. C 4. C 5. E 6. C 7. D*

Game #5: June 1993 Questions 1-5   *1. D 2. B 3. D 4. D 5. A*

Game #6: December 1994 Questions 7-11   *7. E 8. E 9. C 10. C 11. C*

Game #7: June 1995 Questions 1-6   *1. D 2. B 3. C 4. A 5. D 6. A*

Game #8: December 1995 Questions 1-5   *1. E 2. E 3. B 4. B 5. D*

Game #9: June 1996 Questions 1-7   *1. B 2. E 3. C 4. E 5. D 6. D 7. C*

Chapter Three: Advanced Linear Games

Game #1: June 1991 Questions 8-13   *8. B 9. D 10. A 11. B 12. D 13. C*

Game #2: June 1991 Questions 19-24   *19. E 20. A 21. A 22. B 23. E 24. C*

Game #3: October 1991 Questions 18-24   *18. E 19. B 20. E 21. A 22. E 23. B 24. D*

Game #4: December 1991 Questions 14-19   *14. A 15. D 16. D 17. E 18. D 19. A*

Game #5: February 1992 Questions 12-17   *12. B 13. C 14. E 15. A 16. D 17. B*

Game #6: June 1992 Questions 18-24   *18. B 19. C 20. C 21. D 22. A 23. E 24. E*

Game #7: February 1993 Questions 8-12   *8. B 9. C 10. E 11. E 12. E*

Game #8: June 1993 Questions 13-17   *13. C 14. C 15. E 16. B 17. D*

Game #9: February 1995 Questions 19-24   *19. B 20. A 21. C 22. B 23. B 24. C*

Game #10: September 1995 Questions 13-18   *13. D 14. B 15. A 16. A 17. E 18. A*

Game #11: December 1995 Questions 13-17   *13. E 14. D 15. D 16. B 17. B*

Game #12: October 1996 Questions 1-5   *1. A 2. A 3. D 4. A 5. B*

Chapter Four: Grouping Games

Game #1: December 1991 Questions 1-7   *1. D 2. B 3. A 4. E 5. C 6. A 7. D*

Game #2: December 1991 Questions 20-24   *20. B 21. C 22. D 23. B 24. C*

Game #3: February 1992 Questions 7-11   *7. E 8. C 9. A 10. E 11. E*

Game #4: June 1992 Questions 7-11   *7. A 8. B 9. B 10. B 11. D*

Game #5: June 1992 Questions 12-17   *12. B 13. B 14. C 15. C 16. D 17. B*

Game #6: June 1993 Questions 18-24   *18. D 19. B 20. E 21. D 22. B 23. E 24. C*

Game #7: October 1993 Questions 8-13   *8. D 9. B 10. B 11. B 12. C 13. E*

Game #8: June 1994 Questions 1-6   *1. A 2. E 3. B 4. D 5. C 6. B*

Game #9: June 1994 Questions 12-19   *12. D 13. C 14. E 15. B 16. A 17. C 18. A 19. C*

Game #10: October 1994 Questions 7-11   *7. E 8. A 9. E 10. D 11. B*

Game #11: October 1994 Questions 12-17   *12. D 13. B 14. B 15. A 16. C 17. C*

Game #12: December 1994 Questions 1-6   *1. D 2. B 3. C 4. E 5. B 6. D*

Game #13: February 1995 Questions 1-6   *1. B 2. A 3. E 4. B 5. D 6. C*

Game #14: February 1995 Questions 13-18   *13. D 14. D 15. D 16. D 17. B 18. E*

Game #15: June 1995 Questions 20-24   *20. C 21. C 22. B 23. A 24. A*

Game #16: September 1995 Questions 1-6   *1. D 2. E 3. A 4. E 5. C 6. D*

Game #17: December 1995 Questions 6-12   *6. D 7. C 8. B 9. E 10. E 11. E 12. B*

Game #18: December 1992 Questions 1-6   *1. C 2. D 3. D 4. A 5. C 6. E*

Game #19: December 1992 Questions 20-24   *20. E 21. D 22. B 23. E 24. B*

Game #20: June 1996 Questions 13-19   *13. C 14. E 15. C 16. A 17. B 18. A 19. B*

Game #21: June 1996 Questions 20-24   *20. E 21. A 22. C 23. D 24. A*

Game #22: October 1996 Questions 6-12   *6. A 7. E 8. B 9. A 10. A 11. C 12. E*

Chapter Five: Grouping/Linear Combination Games

Game #1: February 1994 Questions 19-24   *19.* B *20.* C *21.* E *22.* B *23.* D *24.* A

Game #2: December 1994 Questions 12-17   *12.* B *13.* A *14.* E *15.* D *16.* B *17.* E

Game #3: October 1996 Questions 19-24   *19.* E *20.* C *21.* D *22.* D *23.* B *24.* C

Chapter Six: Pure Sequencing Games

Game #1: June 1991 Questions 14-18   *14.* C *15.* E *16.* D *17.* B *18.* D

Game #2: October 1991 Questions 1-5   *1.* D *2.* A *3.* A *4.* E *5.* D

Game #3: February 1992 Questions 1-6   *1.* D *2.* C *3.* D *4.* D *5.* C *6.* D

Game #4: October 1992 Questions 7-12   *7.* C *8.* E *9.* C *10.* A *11.* B *12.* B

Game #5: February 1994 Questions 1-5   *1.* B *2.* C *3.* C *4.* C *5.* E

Chapter Seven: The Forgotten Few Games

Game #1: October 1993 Questions 14-18   *14.* D *15.* B *16.* B *17.* C *18.* D

Game #2: February 1994 Questions 13-18   *13.* B *14.* D *15.* C *16.* D *17.* E *18.* C

Game #3: December 1994 Questions 18-24   *18.* E *19.* C *20.* A *21.* A *22.* D *23.* C *24.* E

Game #4: September 1995 Questions 19-24   *19.* D *20.* E *21.* A *22.* C *23.* A *24.* C

Game #5: October 1996 Questions 13-18   *13.* C *14.* D *15.* C *16.* E *17.* E *18.* D

Game #6: June 1991 Questions 1-7   *1.* B *2.* A *3.* B *4.* E *5.* E *6.* C *7.* E

Game #7: October 1992 Questions 13-19   *13.* E *14.* A *15.* D *16.* A *17.* D *18.* B *19.* C

Game #8: October 1992 Questions 20-24   *20.* D *21.* C *22.* B *23.* B *24.* A

Game #9: October 1993 Questions 19-24   *19.* E *20.* A *21.* D *22.* D *23.* B *24.* A

Game #10: June 1995 Questions 7-13   *7.* D *8.* A *9.* E *10.* E *11.* D *12.* E *13.* A

Game #11: December 1992 Questions 14-19   *14.* C *15.* C *16.* A *17.* C *18.* E *19.* A

Chapter Eight: Advanced Features and Techniques Games

Game #1: October 1991 Questions 13-17   *13. A 14. D 15. D 16. B 17. C*

Game #2: February 1992 Questions 18-24   *18. E 19. C 20. D 21. A 22. A 23. C 24. B*

Game #3: October 1992 Questions 1-6   *1. A 2. D 3. C 4. D 5. E 6. D*

Game #4: February 1993 Questions 13-18   *13. B 14. C 15. E 16. A 17. E 18. B*

Game #5: February 1993 Questions 19-24   *19. E 20. D 21. B 22. D 23. B 24. A*

Game #6: June 1993 Questions 6-12   *6. C 7. B 8. B 9. D 10. A 11. B 12. E*

Game #7: October 1993 Questions 1-7   *1. C 2. D 3. B 4. A 5. C 6. D 7. A*

Game #8: February 1994 Questions 6-12   *6. A 7. E 8. E 9. E 10. B 11. C 12. B*

Game #9: June 1994 Questions 7-11   *7. B 8. D 9. B 10. B 11. D*

Game #10: June 1994 Questions 20-24   *20. E 21. E 22. A 23. B 24. A*

Game #11: October 1994 Questions 1-6   *1. E 2. B 3. C 4. B 5. C 6. D*

Game #12: October 1994 Questions 18-24   *18. D 19. C 20. B 21. A 22. E 23. E 24. D*

Game #13: February 1995 Questions 7-12   *7. E 8. A 9. B 10. C 11. E 12. A*

Game #14: June 1995 Questions 14-19   *14. D 15. E 16. C 17. A 18. B 19. E*

Game #15: September 1995 Questions 7-12   *7. E 8. B 9. C 10. E 11. C 12. B*

Game #16: December 1995 Questions 18-24   *18. A 19. D 20. E 21. C 22. C 23. B 24. B*

Game #17: December 1992 Questions 7-13   *7. D 8. A 9. B 10. D 11. B 12. E 13. C*

Game #18: June 1996 Questions 8-12   *8. B 9. C 10. A 11. A 12. C*

APPENDIX

Test-by-Test Game Classification and Location Identifier

This section contains a reverse lookup that references every game in this book according to the source LSAT. The tests are listed in order of PrepTest number, from PrepTest 1 (June 1991) to PrepTest 20 (October 1996). All other Law Services publication identifiers are also listed. Each game is classified according to the proprietary PowerScore LSAT Logic Games Classification system. Thereafter, the chapter, and page number where each game can be found in this book is listed.

The classification can be used to identify the four games that appeared on each LSAT PrepTest, and to help you understand the composition of each LSAT Games section. If you choose, you can use this lookup to find the four games from an individual test and then do those four games in order, re-creating that test section.

Game   **Game Type**   **Book Location**

June 1991 (LSAT PrepTest 1)

Game #1:   Circular Linearity: Balanced—Chapter 7, page 94
Game #2:   Advanced Linear: Unbalanced: Underfunded—Chapter 3, page 37
Game #3:   Pure Sequencing—Chapter 6, page 81
Game #4:   Advanced Linear: Unbalanced: Underfunded—Chapter 3, page 38

October 1991 (LSAT PrepTest 2; LSAT TriplePrep, Volume 1)

Game #1:   Pure Sequencing—Chapter 6, page 82
Game #2:   Basic Linear: Unbalanced: Overloaded—Chapter 2, page 25
Game #3:   Pure Numerical Distribution—Chapter 8, page 103
Game #4:   Advanced Linear: Balanced—Chapter 3, page 39

December 1991 (LSAT PrepTest 3; LSAT TriplePrep, Volume 2)

Game #1:   Grouping: Defined-Fixed, Unbalanced: Underfunded—Chapter 4, page 51
Game #2:   Basic Linear: Balanced—Chapter 2, page 26
Game #3:   Advanced Linear: Balanced—Chapter 3, page 40
Game #4:   Grouping: Partially Defined—Chapter 4, page 52

February 1992 (LSAT PrepTest 4; LSAT TriplePrep, Volume 1)

Game #1:   Pure Sequencing—Chapter 6, page 83
Game #2:   Grouping: Defined-Fixed, Unbalanced: Underfunded—Chapter 4, page 53
Game #3:   Advanced Linear: Balanced—Chapter 3, page 41
Game #4:   Mapping-Supplied Diagram, Identify the Possibilities—Chapter 8, page 104

June 1992 (LSAT PrepTest 5; LSAT TriplePrep, Volume 1)

Game #1: Basic Linear: Undefined—Chapter 2, page 27
Game #2: Grouping: Defined-Fixed, Unbalanced: Overloaded—Chapter 4, page 54
Game #3: Grouping: Defined-Fixed, Unbalanced: Overloaded—Chapter 4, page 55
Game #4: Advanced Linear: Balanced—Chapter 3, page 42

October 1992 (LSAT PrepTest 6; LSAT TriplePrep, Volume 2)

Game #1: Grouping: Defined-Moving, Balanced, Numerical Distribution—Chapter 8, page 105
Game #2: Pure Sequencing—Chapter 6, page 84
Game #3: Mapping-Supplied Diagram, Directional—Chapter 7, page 95
Game #4: Mapping-Spatial Relations (This could classified as a Grouping game: the map has little impact since the bridges are not straight.)—Chapter 7, page 96

December 1992 (LSAT PrepTest 18; 10 Actual, Official LSAT PrepTests)

Game #1: Grouping: Defined-Fixed, Balanced—Chapter 4, page 68
Game #2: Basic Linear: Balanced, Identify the Templates—Chapter 8, page 119
Game #3: Mapping- Spatial Relations—Chapter 7, page 99
Game #4: Grouping: Partially Defined—Chapter 4, page 69

February 1993 (LSAT PrepTest 7; LSAT TriplePrep, Volume 2; 10 Actual, Official LSAT PrepTests)

Game #1: Basic Linear: Balanced—Chapter 2, page 28
Game #2: Advanced Linear: Balanced—Chapter 3, page 43
Game #3: Grouping: Defined-Moving, Balanced, Numerical Distribution—Chapter 8, page 106
Game #4: Advanced Linear: Balanced, Identify the Templates—Chapter 8, page 107

June 1993 (LSAT PrepTest 8; LSAT TriplePrep, Volume 3)

Game #1: Basic Linear: Unbalanced: Overloaded—Chapter 2, page 29
Game #2: Circular Linearity: Identify the Possibilities—Chapter 8, page 108
Game #3: Advanced Linear: Balanced—Chapter 3, page 44
Game #4: Grouping: Partially Defined—Chapter 4, page 56

October 1993 (LSAT PrepTest 9; LSAT TriplePrep, Volume 3; 10 Actual, Official LSAT PrepTests)

Game #1: Grouping: Defined-Fixed, Unbalanced: Underfunded, Numerical Distribution—Chapter 8, page 109
Game #2: Grouping: Defined-Fixed, Unbalanced: Overloaded—Chapter 4, page 57
Game #3: Pattern—Chapter 7, page 89
Game #4: Mapping-Supplied Diagram (Like many Mapping games this one has strong grouping elements.)—Chapter 7, page 97

February 1994 (LSAT PrepTest 10; LSAT TriplePrep, Volume 3; 10 Actual, Official LSAT PrepTests)

Game #1: Pure Sequencing—Chapter 6, page 85
Game #2: Basic Linear: Unbalanced: Overloaded, Numerical Distribution, Identify the Possibilities—Chapter 8, page 110
Game #3: Pattern—Chapter 7, page 90
Game #4: Grouping/Linear Combination—Chapter 5, page 75

June 1994 (LSAT PrepTest 11; LSAT TriplePrep Plus with Explanations; 10 Actual, Official LSAT PrepTests)

Game #1: Grouping: Defined-Moving, Balanced—Chapter 4, page 58
Game #2: Basic Linear: Balanced to Unbalanced: Underfunded, Numerical Distribution—Chapter 8, page 111
Game #3: Grouping: Defined-Moving, Unbalanced: Overloaded—Chapter 4, page 59
Game #4: Pattern: Identify the Possibilities—Chapter 8, page 112

October 1994 (LSAT PrepTest 12; LSAT TriplePrep Plus with Explanations; 10 Actual, Official LSAT PrepTests)

Game #1: Basic Linear: Balanced, Identify the Possibilities—Chapter 8, page 113
Game #2: Grouping: Defined-Fixed, Balanced—Chapter 4, page 60
Game #3: Grouping: Partially Defined—Chapter 4, page 61
Game #4: Pattern: Identify the Possibilities—Chapter 8, page 114

December 1994 (LSAT PrepTest 13; LSAT TriplePrep Plus with Explanations; 10 Actual, Official LSAT PrepTests)

Game #1: Grouping: Defined-Fixed, Balanced—Chapter 4, page 62
Game #2: Basic Linear: Balanced—Chapter 2, page 30
Game #3: Grouping/Linear Combination—Chapter 5, page 76
Game #4: Pattern—Chapter 7, page 91

February 1995 (LSAT PrepTest 14; 10 Actual, Official LSAT PrepTests)

Game #1: Grouping: Defined-Moving, Balanced—Chapter 4, page 63
Game #2: Advanced Linear: Balanced, Identify the Templates—Chapter 8, page 115
Game #3: Grouping: Partially Defined—Chapter 4, page 64
Game #4: Advanced Linear: Unbalanced: Overloaded—Chapter 3, page 45

June 1995 (LSAT PrepTest 15; 10 Actual, Official LSAT PrepTests)

Game #1: Basic Linear: Balanced—Chapter 2, page 31
Game #2: Mapping   (Again, one with strong grouping elements.)—Chapter 7, page 98
Game #3: Basic Linear: Unbalanced: Underfunded, Numerical Distribution—Chapter 8, page 116
Game #4: Grouping: Defined-Fixed, Unbalanced: Overloaded—Chapter 4, page 65

September 1995 (LSAT PrepTest 16; 10 Actual, Official LSAT PrepTests)

Game #1: Grouping: Defined-Fixed, Balanced—Chapter 4, page 66
Game #2: Advanced Linear: Balanced, Identify the Templates—Chapter 8, page 117
Game #3: Advanced Linear: Unbalanced: Underfunded—Chapter 3, page 46
Game #4: Pattern—Chapter 7, page 92

December 1995 (LSAT PrepTest 17)

Game #1: Basic Linear: Balanced—Chapter 2, page 32
Game #2: Grouping: Defined-Fixed, Unbalanced: Underfunded—Chapter 4, page 67
Game #3: Advanced Linear: Unbalanced: Overloaded—Chapter 3, page 47
Game #4: Advanced Linear: Balanced, Identify the Possibilities—Chapter 8, page 118

June 1996 (LSAT PrepTest 19; 10 More Actual, Official LSAT PrepTests)

Game #1: Basic Linear: Balanced—Chapter 2, page 33
Game #2: Advanced Linear: Balanced, Numerical Distribution, Identify the Templates—Chapter 8, page 120
Game #3: Grouping: Defined-Fixed, Balanced—Chapter 4, page 70
Game #4: Grouping: Defined-Fixed, Balanced—Chapter 4, page 71

October 1996 (PrepTest 20; 10 More Actual, Official LSAT PrepTests; The Official LSAT Sample PrepTest—free online

Game #1: Advanced Linear: Unbalanced: Underfunded—Chapter 3, page 48
Game #2: Grouping: Defined-Fixed, Unbalanced: Overloaded—Chapter 4, page 72
Game #3: Pattern—Chapter 7, page 93
Game #4: Grouping/Linear Combination—Chapter 5, page 77

LSAT Classification Notes:

1. The December 1993 LSAT was nondisclosed. It was later administered as the September 1995 LSAT and then released as PrepTest 16.

2. Starting in 1996, the February LSATs have been nondisclosed. In April 2000, the February 1997 LSAT was released as the Official LSAT PrepTest with Explanations, Volume One. In May 2004, the February 1996, February 1999, and February 2000 LSATs were released in The Official LSAT SuperPrep.